52 Wisconsin Weekends

52 Wisconsin Weekends

GREAT GETAWAYS AND ADVENTURES FOR EVERY SEASON

THIRD EDITION

BOB PUHALA

COUNTRY ROADS PRESS

NTC/Contemporary Publishing Group

Library of Congress Cataloging-in-Publication Data

Puhala, Bob.
    52 Wisconsin weekends : great getaways and adventures for every
season / Bob Puhala. — 3rd ed.
       p.   cm. — (52 weekends)
    Includes index.
    ISBN 1-56626-027-2
    1. Wisconsin Guidebooks.   I. Title.   II. Title: Fifty-two
Wisconsin weekends.
    F579.3.P84   1999
    917.7504′43—dc21
                                   99-29876
                                         CIP

Cover and interior design by Nick Panos
Cover and interior illustrations copyright © Jill Banashek
Map by Mapping Specialists, Madison, Wisconsin
Picture research by Elizabeth Broadrup Lieberman and Jill Birschbach

Published by Country Roads Press
A division of NTC/Contemporary Publishing Group, Inc.
4255 West Touhy Avenue, Lincolnwood (Chicago), Illinois 60712-1975 U.S.A.
Copyright © 2000, 1997, 1994 by Bob Puhala
Printed in the United States of America
International Standard Book Number: 1-56626-027-2
00 01 02 03 04 05 QV 18 17 16 15 14 13 12 11 10 9 8 7 6 5 4 3 2 1

For my Wisconsin travel buddies—
Kate, Dayne, Debbie, Ma, Pa—love ya'all!

MINNESOTA

Lake Superior

APOSTLE ISLANDS

Bayfield

MICHIGAN

Hayward

St. Germain

Couderay

Chetek

Merrill

White Lake

Green Bay

DOOR COUNTY

WISCONSIN

Mississippi

River

Appleton

Oshkosh

Manitowoc

Fond du Lac

Kohler

Wisconsin Dells

North Freedom   Baraboo

Horicon

Prairie du Sac

Cedarburg

Spring Green

Ashippun

Hubertus

Prairie
du Chien

Madison

Blue Mounds

Cambridge

West
Allis

Milwaukee

Lake Michigan

Mount Horeb

Platteville

Mineral
Point

New Glarus

Eagle

Racine

Delavan

Lake
Geneva

IOWA

ILLINOIS

INDIANA

Contents

Fall

 # Winter

Introduction

I'VE GOT THE BIGGEST BACKYARD IN THE MIDWEST. IT'S called Wisconsin.

At least that's how this Chicago native thinks of the Dairy State. My earliest memories of family vacations include fishing trips to Minocqua, lumberjack shows in Hayward, touring by car along the Mississippi River near La Crosse, and boat rides on Lake Geneva.

I also have roots in Wisconsin. My uncle owned a dairy farm in Lublin. On visits there, I'd help feed the animals, bale hay, and harvest corn. We'd sit down to incredible breakfasts of steak, eggs, potatoes, veggies, fresh home-baked bread, and more. At night, we'd laze on the farm-house porch, talk about baseball, and gaze at a starlit sky.

When my grandmother was nearly 80, she moved from our near west-side apartment building in Chicago onto a 250-acre farmstead in Mountain. It included pasture, meadows, timberland, and its own private lake. Imagine my surprise the first time we visited Grandma and she greeted us wearing a big straw hat. Just like that, after more than a half century in Chicago, she had gone native.

I remember when we came "this close" to purchasing a log cabin on 14 acres near Crivitz, complete with its own private trout stream. The entire family took a long weekend's drive to this north woods outpost, fell in love with the place, only to be sorely disappointed when it was sold out from under us. We're still looking for that perfect weekend getaway, but nothing quite measures up to that long-ago cabin.

However, it didn't take vacations to bring us to Wisconsin. Almost every Saturday during my elementary and high school years, Pa would wake me up at the crack of dawn, shake me out of bed. Then we'd make a quick breakfast, get in the car, point it toward the Wisconsin border, and hit the road. Most of the time, we didn't even decide where we were going until we got there.

During my college years Devil's Lake became a favorite spot of mine. I loved to go rock climbing on the high bluffs that surround the glacial lake. Still do.

And let's not forget the Wisconsin State Fair, always a family tradition. Hot buttered corn, cream puffs, livestock shows. During the 1970s I even managed to convince my parents to attend a grandstand concert featuring Foreigner, then a popular rock band. We stayed for the entire show, but my pa spent the evening with fingers in his ears.

My first Midwest press trip as a professional travel journalist was made to Wisconsin. We visited the historic fishing village of Bayfield and the Apostle Islands. I wrote a good story, made some great friends, and drank locally made cherry wine. Well, two out of three ain't bad.

I even met my wife in Wisconsin.

Prowling Door County to do a ski-season preview article, I spotted this gorgeous woman getting an ice cream cone at Wilson's in Ephraim. It was too crowded to talk; I could only smile across the room. Then she left.

Later, I'd wandered into a Fish Creek restaurant to get some dinner and watch the Cubs play the Padres in the 1984 playoffs. The place was packed, and there was only one open chair at the bar where I was watching a big-screen TV play out the Cubbies' sad tale. You guessed it. Debbie walked in with a girlfriend, had to wait for a dinner table, and plunked down on the seat next to me.

"Is anybody sitting here?" she asked.

"Uh-uh," I said, trying to concentrate on the game.

"Mind if I sit here?" she asked again.

"Uh-uh," I said, trying to concentrate on the game.

"Are you a Cubs fan?" she asked a third time.

"Uh-huh," I said, trying to concentrate on the game.

Apparently my charming demeanor intrigued her.

We did actually start to talk, and I invited myself to breakfast the next morning. Before she left "the Door" later that day, I asked her to go to a Blackhawks game with me back in Chicago. The rest, as they say, is history.

Debbie is a Wisconsin lover, too. There isn't a month goes by that she doesn't suggest we sneak away to the American Club in Kohler, perhaps her favorite Midwest getaway.

Our daughters, Kate and Dayne, continue the family tradition as Wisconsin boosters. They live and breathe for a summer ramble to Wisconsin Dells, love running on Door County beaches, and can't pass up the cream puffs at the Wisconsin State Fair.

Wisconsin is special to me—the last great escape, as I like to call it, in the Midwest. I hope it becomes special for you, too.

How to Use This Book

I'VE CHOSEN SOME OF THE STATE'S BEST GETAWAYS, FESTIVALS, events, and activities for *52 Wisconsin Weekends*. They are listed seasonally (spring, summer, fall, winter); however, several of the weekends can be enjoyed regardless of the season. So treat the order as a guide, and decide for yourself when is the best time for you to take these trips.

Great effort has been taken to provide the information that will make your trip most enjoyable, including historical elements and background information as insights into a destination's character. Although all information was checked and updated before going to press, it is important to *call ahead* before leaving home. Make sure that the attraction or hotel is open, that activities continue to be offered. Check on schedules or hours. That way you'll never be disappointed.

It is equally important that you *confirm* dates and times of special festivals and events. Festivals can be canceled; events might be postponed. Dates can flipflop from one year to another.

52 Wisconsin Weekends is also full of specific tips and helpful hints for you to enjoy your outing. However, most chapters do not offer recommendations for lodging or restaurants. You can contact the local chamber of commerce, ask a friend, or rely on locals' favorites for these—people are always willing to share the best of their hometowns.

Please note: People do not pay to be included in this guidebook! I have chosen all entries, based on three decades of traveling the state and 15 years' experience as a professional travel journalist. If you have a favorite weekend getaway that I haven't included in the book, drop me a note. I'd be happy to discover some of your gems, too.

Important! One last caution is that Midwest area codes, like those in other parts of the country, undergo frequent and confusing changes. Although every effort has been made to provide you with accurate phone numbers, future changes could cause glitches. So . . . if you dial an attraction's phone number and the call does not go through, here's the easy way to obtain the new telephone number: dial 1, then the area code you have for the attraction, *then* 555-1212. This will get you an area directory-assistance operator. Tell him or her the city, state, and name of the attraction. You'll then receive the correct area code and telephone number. And if you still need information, you can always call Wisconsin Tourism at 800-432-8747.

Spring

1

Mountain Biking

MERRILL

As we thundered along the Underdown, a wilderness mountain-bike trail hidden deep in the backwoods of northern Wisconsin, my brother Mark suddenly skidded to a stop.

"Are these what I think they are?" he asked.

"Yep," I answered. "Bear tracks. No doubt about it."

"How big, Grizzly Adams?" he asked, using his favorite outdoorsman nickname for me, which, incidently, drove me crazy.

"About the size of a Volkswagen," I guessed. "But don't sweat it. Even if we actually see one in the flesh, and that'd be pretty rare for midday, it'd probably just run away."

"Probably is the operative word in that sentence," Mark said. But we continued blithely on for nearly three and one-half hours along 21 miles of trails that have been called "possibly the best off-road riding in the state."

The Underdown, located about nine miles north of Merrill, gets its moniker from namesake Bill, a legendary moonshiner who buried his still operations deep in these hills during Prohibition days. Today, it's as inaccessible to civilization as it was back in the era of marauding G-men looking for illegal booze shacks.

Its narrow, rolling trails boast all the best ingredients for fat-tire fun. We tracked our 21-speed, lightweight aluminum-frame bikes up and down impossibly steep, winding forest hills; around sharp turns; through yards-long, muddy holes and gooey marsh-slop holes; over pothole boulders; and along several meadows stripped bare for deer-yards in winter.

In all our time spent on the trail, we didn't see another human being. That's why it's important that anybody tackling the Underdown be armed with trail maps, compass, and plenty of water. Even though these bike trails follow cross-country ski routes marked at irregular intervals, it's easy to get lost out here. Lincoln County extension officials report that during winter, the ski patrol sweeps the trails at the end of each day and regularly comes up with stragglers. Same thing can happen to summer revelers.

Besides rigorous exercise, the Underdown offers a wonderland of natural beauty. Bike trails are lined with dainty purple violets, tall black-eyed Susans, and large oxeye daisies. Fragrant water lilies float platter-like on lakes and ponds, blooming through September. Wild fruits include blackberry, chokecherry, and strawberry, but don't pick or eat anything unless you're absolutely sure what it is. And everything from giant white pine and northern red oak to white birch and eastern hemlock grows haphazardly in the dense forests.

Be forewarned that in summer the Underdown is a haven for swarms of insects, including ticks. So despite temps in the 60s during our fat-tire ramble, we slopped our bodies with bug dope. Insects still treated us as if we were human entrées on some "bite 'em, suck 'em" critter menu from hell.

Another excellent, albeit much tamer, off-road bike trail is the Bearskin, stretching 18 miles over an abandoned railroad grade between Minocqua and Oneida County Highway K, its southern trailhead. But don't get the wrong idea. The

Bearskin remains a genuine wilderness jaunt, traveling over a number of old railroad trestles that span lakes and creeks, as well as offering stretches of up to five miles where you'll see no houses or people other than a few fellow bikers.

It would be unusual if at sometime during your 18-mile trip you do not see an eagle; nearly 65 percent of the 428 eagles in Wisconsin make their summer homes in the high pines of these forests. You're also likely to hear the distinctive wail of the common loon, the red-eyed bird that can dive into lake waters and remain submerged for up to 10 minutes.

The trail skirts several logging and railroad ghost towns, pedals near beaver dams and lodges, and passes woodlands filled with quaking aspen, whose slender silver leaves quiver in the slightest breeze.

South of Goodnow you cross the Bearskin's longest trestle, 746 feet long across a marshy bog. More than 100 years ago a steam locomotive and three cars derailed here, falling into the bog on the west side of the trestle. Two huge cranes were brought in to fish out the equipment; one crane tipped and fell into the muck, too. That wrapped up the salvage efforts. It's said that if you poke a 20-foot steel rod through the moss, water, and muck even today, you'll hit the engine resting on the bottom.

Our pedal-pushing sojourn also took us to Langlade County, whose vast potential for off-road biking adventures has hardly been tapped. In fact, the county owns nearly 125,000 acres of timberlands for mountain bikers wanting a challenge.

We headed to the Parrish Hills, west of Elcho and about 12 miles north of Antigo, for really rugged riding along the vast network of logging trails that wind through the middle of pure wilderness. These trails are not marked, so be sure to bring a compass along. Here were more bear tracks, along with raccoon and deer markings; I even got stuck in an

Mountain Biking

ankle-deep mud puddle. We traveled through an eerie tunnel of trees that had me thinking about scary *Twilight Zone* episodes. And lots of trail forks offered plenty of opportunities to get lost.

Lacking a compass, conversations during our 26-mile jaunt went something like this:

"Hey Mark, do you remember if we turned off at this deadfall or that one?"

"I'm not sure. I thought you were keeping track of where we're going."

"Well, I'm not."

"Neither am I."

We also tried some mountain-bike bushwhacking along Jack Lake's trail, about eight miles north of Antigo. This cross-country ski path is neither marked nor maintained in summer, and, as a result, brush and weeds rose as tall as our knees as we sat on our bikes. After riding through a few miles of incredibly buggy terrain, Mark called out, "I sure wish I had my .357 with me."

"Still thinking about the bears?" I asked.

"For the mosquitos," he said.

For More Information

Off-road biking fests include the Merrill Colorama Bike Tour, held annually at the end of September; choose from a 30-mile or 50-mile scenic tour. Call 715-536-7313.

A free set of four detailed bike maps is available from the Wisconsin Division of Tourism, which include paved, off-road, and mountain bike trails. Call 800-432-8747.

You can rent mountain bikes from area outfitters, but be sure they are lightweight and relatively new for dependability. We had excellent bikes from Scotty's, in Tomahawk.

Rates include half-day and weekly rentals. Call 715-453-1888.

To get more information on mountain biking in northern Wisconsin and the above activities and events, for Underdown and Lincoln County contact Merrill Chamber of Commerce, 201 North Center Avenue, Merrill, WI 54452, 715-536-9474; for Langlade County contact the Chamber of Commerce, P.O. Box 339, Superior Street, Antigo, WI 54409, 715-627-6236.

Mountain Biking

2

Wisconsin Waterfalls

IN RUGGED NORTHERN WISCONSIN, ANNUAL SPRING STORMS combine with melting winter snows to swell inland rivers and stir some into swirling white-water maelstroms feeding waterfalls. No one knows exactly how many waterfalls grace the Wisconsin landscape. Many are spectacular, others gently romantic. Rapids, chutes, dales, cascades, gorges— together they create magnificent water sculptures carved deep in wilderness forests. At least 20 falls dot four contiguous counties (Douglas, Bayfield, Ashland, and Iron) that hug Lake Superior, forming the heart of Wisconsin's "waterfall country."

If you're a weekender who loves to hike and explore backwoods and back roads, here's a guide to some of the state's most magical waterfalls.

The tallest (and the fourth highest east of the Rocky Mountains) is Big Manitou Falls, which tumbles 165 feet down a gorge carved by the Black River. Located in Pattison State Park, 15 miles south of Superior, it was formed like many others in the region: by rivers dropping onto the Lake Superior lowlands and tumbling on down to the lake itself. Just a few days of spring rains can greatly increase the water volume in these streams, creating rushing waterfalls.

A footbridge vista leads to the head of Big Manitou. For

the more adventurous, a cantilevered overlook hangs over the gorge; from here you'll see the entire falls system plus sprawling lowlands to the north that separate the park from steeply rising bluffs in Duluth, Minnesota.

The falls were a gathering place named by the Ojibwa Indians, who believed they could hear the voice of the Great Spirit in the roar of the waters. They held the water in such reverence that they were reluctant to peer over the edge for fear of offending the spirits.

Around the base of the falls are gaping holes dug into the sides of sheer cliffs. These former copper mines date back to Northwest Fur Company's explorations in the 1850s.

About a mile upstream is Little Manitou Falls, which drops only 31 feet. The Indians called this stretch "Laughing Rapids" because of the murmur the water makes going over the rocks. Near the river is Interfalls Lake, with the finest area beach. A third waterfall, Copper Creek, is located in a remote section of the park.

About 25 miles northeast is Amnicon Falls State Park with its twin waterfalls. The park's most spectacular vista is a quarter-mile island reached by a covered bridge between the falls on the Amnicon River. Water tumbles 25 feet over exposed lava rock. Hiking trails and overlooks follow the river's rapids system.

Farther east, Ashland County's Copper Falls State Park boasts its namesake Copper Falls, where the Bad River plunges more than 40 feet into a narrow gorge, and Brownstone Falls, a 30-foot drop on the Tyler Forks. Footbridges cross these steep gorges to give spirited views of the falls.

Morgan Falls, reached from a ranger access road in the Chequamegon National Forest, is the third-largest in the state, plunging nearly 100 feet into a tributary of Morgan Creek.

In the northeast, Marinette County boasts at least 14 waterfalls, mostly nestled in its interior woods. A sentimental favorite might be Dave's Falls, located in a county park near Amberg and named for a logging hero who gave his life while freeing a logjam on the Pike River.

For More Information

For waterfall listings and state park admission or fee information, contact the Wisconsin Department of Natural Resources, Bureau of Parks and Recreation, P.O. Box 7921, Madison, WI 53707, 608-266-2181. Another information source is the Wisconsin Department of Development, Division of Tourism, 123 West Washington Avenue, Madison, WI 53707, 608-266-2161 or 800-372-2737.

Wisconsin Waterfalls

3

"Little Soho"

MILWAUKEE

THE HISTORIC THIRD WARD IS MILWAUKEE'S OWN LITTLE Soho, a relatively undiscovered jumble of art galleries, boutiques, cafés, and coffee shops located in an old warehouse district just a short walk from downtown.

Bordered by the harbor, the Milwaukee River, and the central business district, the Third Ward was a ghostly shambles little more than two decades ago, when most of its wholesalers fled Water, Broadway, and Milwaukee streets. But pioneering entrepreneurs led the charge toward a neighborhood renaissance; after more than 20 years of tireless work and self-promotion, the historic Third Ward has earned a reputation as one of the city's most innovative and creative meccas for artists, photographers, clothing designers, and others. Hundreds of abandoned warehouses have been transformed into chic loft offices, galleries, and apartments.

The best way to explore the Third Ward is by parking your car and walking around the neighborhood. Among some of my personal favorites my first stop is always an eclectic upscale boutique at 241 North Broadway called Eccola, an Italian word that translates to "here it is." That's right on target, for this bizarre bazaar offers everything from primitive African art, life-size plaster cupids, and freeze-dried rattlesnakes to holstein-cow Christmas lights, glass tables supported by faux elephant tusks, and high-tech curiosities.

Creative merchandise displays help make the boutique's customers feel they're wandering through a museum rather than a retail store. Oddities range in price from pocket change to hundreds of dollars. My last purchase here was an authentic Afghanistani freedom-fighter hat for $14.

Then I stroll to La Boulangerie, at 233 North Broadway. The café on the lower level boasts great homemade muffins, wonderful breads, and decadent pastries. It has also become a popular hangout for local politicians, especially during breakfast and lunch hours.

Switch gears at White Thunder Wolf, 306 North Milwaukee, home to a large selection of Native American arts and crafts. Especially popular are dream catchers, large redwood hoops surrounding intricate nets adorned with feathers. Other mystical items include coyote-teeth necklaces, jewelry, and even watchballs—blown-glass globes inhabited by "protective creatures" that ward off bad spirits.

Antique hunters gravitate to the Milwaukee Antique Center, 341 North Milwaukee. It's Wisconsin's oldest antiques mall, founded in 1974 and boasting three floors of antiques and collectibles. Another browser's paradise is Water Street Antiques, 318 North Water Street, whose 14 dealers boast some of the city's finest antique furniture and oriental rugs.

Don't worry if you get hungry in the Third Ward; you've got plenty of choices. Shakers, 422 South Second, offers everything from Italian pasta to Spanish seafood. The Third Ward Café, 225 East St. Paul, is perhaps the area's best known restaurant, serving Italian specialties; the Broadway Bar & Grill, 233 North Broadway, is a neighborhood tavern established in 1946 and still going strong.

Of course, there are lots of other things going on here: leather stores, piano galleries, dance companies, boutiques, and the renowned avant-garde Theatre X. You can attend gallery-crawl weekends on occasional dates spread throughout the year, and "A Christmas in the Ward," the annual old-fashioned holiday celebration, celebrates with strolling carolers, roasted chestnuts, neighborhood sleigh rides, visits with Santa, and more.

FOR MORE INFORMATION

Contact Historic Third Ward Association, 219 North Milwaukee Street, Milwaukee, WI 53202, 414-273-1173.

"Little Soho"

4

Al Capone's Hideout

COUDERAY

All right, youse guys. Listen up, see. I'm going to lead you to da boss's place right now. So leave your heaters behind. And don't do no talking unless you mugs are spoken to, get it?

AL CAPONE EVENTUALLY GOT IT—A CELL AT ALCATRAZ IN 1932 after being convicted of income tax evasion.

But for several years before this gangster known as Scarface became the new kid at the Big House, he avoided G-men and nasty underworld figures by barricading himself at his north woods retreat, now hidden deep in the woods just six miles north of Couderay.

"He came up here to escape from the business of killing people," says current Capone-house owner Jean Houston. "He was just trying to relax."

Capone, perhaps America's most notorious gangster, built this gangland hideout in the mid-1920s for a then-whopping $250,000; it came complete with special features that transformed it more into an underworld fortress rather than a summer cottage.

His estate covered 500 acres of mostly barren land. "Remember, that was the end of the logging period in Wisconsin," Houston says. "There were no trees at all around here. Everything was wide open for miles and miles."

The main lodge, constructed of native stone and built on a hill overlooking a small lake, was located at the end of a long, gated driveway. About 200 feet from the front door, on the property's tallest hill, a tall gun tower guarded access to the house. Mobsters brandishing tommy guns were always on duty when Scarface was "relaxing" at the estate. From their lofty position "they could see anybody coming near the place," Houston says.

The lodge itself is an impressive building. It has a massive fireplace made from 100 tons of handcut stone; two unique spiral staircases (custom-made of imported mahogany for Capone in Chicago) leading to the house's balcony; and some of his original furnishings, including the boss's desk, chair, and poker table.

"The house looks just like it did when Capone lived here," Houston says. That includes walls 18 inches thick that could withstand any firepower the Feds or rival gangland leaders might direct his way.

Capone left nothing to chance. He had workmen install a light switch in his master bedroom that allowed him to floodlight the entire estate grounds with the flick of a switch, Houston notes. He built an eight-car garage that would conceal mob limousines, which roared in and out of the estate at all hours of the day and night. And legend says he had an escape tunnel burrowed under the home to some point on the grounds; however, Houston claims it caved in on itself long ago.

Big Al used the estate frequently before his trouble began with the Internal Revenue Service. He took associates with him out on the lake to fish. He'd play poker in the main house, and nobody dared tease Capone when he donned his funny-looking tank-top bathing suit and took a dip at his private beach.

Locals pretty much left Capone alone during his Wisconsin visits. "He hired neighbor people to build the house," Houston says, "and paid them with cash in hand. Remember, this was the Depression era, so people liked him for that and caused him no trouble. Besides, people up here had no quarrel with Capone. Those troubles were down in Chicago." If you get the chance, ask senior Couderay residents if they remember any of the comings and goings at Big Al's place; some still do.

When Capone died in 1947, the estate changed hands several times until it was purchased by the Houston family in 1959. With so many curious sightseers stopping to get a look at Capone's former hideout (some even boldly peeked into the windows), Houston opened the house for tours.

Today, 40-minute guided tours take viewers through the main living quarters, including Capone's bedroom; through that eight-car garage, now remodeled as a bar and dining room; past the gun tower and the bunkhouse where his sycophant thugs counted sheep; and to the jail cell.

Seems Capone built his own single-person cell surrounded by a small exercise yard with walls 18 inches thick on the estate. "He used it, all right," Houston said. "But don't ask me who was in there. I wasn't here back then." It's ironic that Big Al would build a jail cell on his property only to land inside of one a few years later.

FOR MORE INFORMATION

Tours are offered daily, May through the third weekend in September and on weekends only from mid-September through October. Admission is charged. Capone's place is located 17 miles southeast of Hayward, on County CC. For more information, contact The Hideout, Couderay, WI 54828, 715-945-2746.

5

Houdini Historical Center

"NOT EVEN DEATH CAN HOLD ME," HARRY HOUDINI ONCE bragged. But so far the escape artist hasn't made good on his boast.

For more than 60 consecutive years, Houdini has failed to materialize during the offical Houdini seance, conducted annually on the anniversary of his death at various locations around the United States and attended by many of America's most renowned magicians. In fact, Harry presumably has not uttered a word to anyone since he died and was laid to rest on October 31, 1926, in the bronze casket used in his escape acts.

Complications from a ruptured appendix, caused by a punch in the stomach during backstage high jinks, did him in. However, Houdini has been resurrected in Appleton, Wisconsin, sort of. His hometown, already boasting a Houdini Elementary School, Houdini Plaza, and Houdini Historical Walk, now offers a world-class Houdini exhibit.

Housed in the Outagamie Museum, the Houdini Historical Center's collection first went on view in 1989. It includes more than 300 pairs of handcuffs, leg irons, and manacles used by the master of escape; straightjackets and other tools of his trade; original posters, programs, scrapbooks, and letters; and nearly 150 historical photographs.

The artifacts belong to Sidney H. Radner of Holyoke, Massachusetts, a protégé of Houdini's escape-artist brother, Theodore Hardeen, who fell heir to the collection. Radner used them in his own magic act, but then decided to loan materials to the museum after Appleton began transforming itself into "Houdiniville, USA."

The exhibit allows a fascinating glimpse of the master of illusions and escapes who thrilled presidents, kings, and queens and filled theaters all over the world. It is the most complete interpretation of Houdini's life ever compiled.

A red, velvet-lined display box that Houdini used to lure people into theaters shows he was a master manipulator. It entices would-be customers (and today's museum-goers) with glimpses of Egyptian leg irons, Spanish handcuffs "used on prisoners burned to death in 1600," spiked handcuffs, and the irons used during the hanging of President Garfield's assassin. Who knows whether these are legitimate historical artifacts or simply a product of Houdini's public relations aplomb? But all the hype helped Houdini earn nearly $2,000 per week, an incredible sum in the 1920s.

Consider some of Houdini's most heralded feats, as chronicled by the museum. He broke out of an escape-proof prison in Moscow; leaped handcuffed and loaded with more than 75 pounds of ball and chain into San Francisco Bay; and escaped from a Chinese water-torture box. His signature trick found him escaping from a locked-and-sealed trunk dropped into water while his hands and feet were chained.

Sure to be a Wisconsin favorite is an exhibit detailing a challenge from a publicity-seeking Connecticut dairy, daring Houdini to perform an escape while submerged in 60 gallons of milk and sealed in a huge milk pail. Harry wasn't cowed, accepted the challenge, and escaped without "uddering" a word.

How did he do it? Well, the museum reveals that Houdini possessed incredibly detailed knowledge of locks and restraints, and perhaps the world's greatest collection of keys, picks, and blades. He kept these goodies in numbered bags, and often would discreetly be given the correct key or tool by assistants—even on stage.

In fact, letters in the center's collection note that friends and neighbors remember him, even as a small child, as a "tinkerer." He constantly took mechanical things apart to see how they worked. Locks held a special fascination for him; by the time Houdini moved with his family to Milwaukee at age nine he no longer needed keys. Endless times as a performer, Houdini would be bound, restrained, or chained while stripped naked and his mouth sealed—and he'd still escape. So perhaps his collection of "freedom gadgets" isn't the only answer to his amazing skills.

Appleton's other Houdini sights include Houdini Plaza (College Avenue and Appleton Street), where the four-and-a-half-ton sculpture *Metamorphosis* (named for his famous trunk escape) can be found. The Houdini Walking Tour numbers 15 sites (marked by plaques), pinpointing places of interest such as his birthplace and the Fox River location where his near-drowning as a child inspired his most famous escape routine.

Even though Appleton lays claim as Houdini's birthplace, citing sketchy records that note the birth of Ehrich Weiss (his real name) on April 6, 1874, to the city's first rabbi and his wife, some historians insist Harry's birthplace is Budapest, Hungary. Fittingly, his birthplace is a mystery.

FOR MORE INFORMATION

A small admission fee is charged to visit the Outagamie Museum's Houdini exhibit; the rest of the museum is free. It's open year-round, Tuesday through Sunday, and is located at 330 East College Avenue, Appleton, WI 54911. For hours and information, call 920-735-9370. For other area information, contact Fox Cities Convention & Visitors Bureau, 110 Fox River Drive, Appleton, WI 54915, 920-734-3358.

Houdini Historical Center

6

House on the Rock

SPRING GREEN

THE HOUSE ON THE ROCK IS THE LOUVRE OF ROADSIDE attractions. A sprawling artistic achievement so enormous, so truly bizarre, so fundamentally and theoretically conceptual, it overwhelms, dazzles, astounds, mystifies, and dizzies.

It is spectacular and silly at the same time, housing an anarchic aesthetic gone mad. Billed as "Wisconsin's Number One Tourist Attraction," with more than 500,000 visitors yearly, it transcends similarly touted altars of supercommercialism. Its kinetic delirium leaves visitors reeling from multiple shocks of Dada.

The House on the Rock is the brainstorm of an eccentric, reclusive genius, Alex Jordan. The Madison sculptor, who died in 1989, began construction in 1940 of a grottolike retreat atop Deershelter Rock.

On a 60-foot-tall chimney of rock overlooking the lush floor of the Upland's Wyoming Valley, he built a Frank Lloyd Wright–influenced house of mortar, stone, and timber blending with the valley it crowns. Local lore says he hauled stone and mortar up the outcropping on his back, using rope ladders or climbing the precarious aerie itself.

Jordan opened the house to public tours in 1961 and has added visionary creations to his always-growing complex ever since, including the daring Infinity Room, a walkway

25

vista with glass walls hanging 140 feet over the edge of craggy rock formations. All are crammed with objects he discovered, built, or collected from travels all over the world.

The total effect is a Dada virtuosity of slapstick art (with the idea behind the work holding more importance than the result itself). In fact, sometimes the result can be totally incidental to the brainstorm that created the display.

But Jordan's house also owes its vision to Dada's French cousin, surrealism—with cavernous rooms, flat black walls, and mostly soft lighting that nurtures visitors into the womb of the unconscious.

In fact, the Organ Room, entered through a 17-foot-high devil's head with moveable eyes and giant horns, is similar in vision to the work of an 18th-century artist who developed his style from hallucinations suffered in a bout of high fever.

The room is a dimly lit maw of space with 52-foot-high ceilings, steel walkways, spiral staircases stretching to infinity, and thirteen bridges—many leading to nowhere—not to mention the myriad grand pianos and three of the greatest organ consoles ever built, including one with fifteen manuals and hundreds of stops. This stately room is easily Jordan's masterpiece.

But each room contains its own spiraling expressionism, with thematic imagery distorted by anarchic splashes of random shapes and contours.

Rooms are filled with colors, music, animated figures, artifacts, statues, sculptures, three-dimensional dioramas, steam engines, scaled-down village streets, mechanical banks, taxidermy, porcelain, ivory, brewery and farm equipment, carved wood, and dolls. Priceless treasures and worthless junk, side by side, make a pointed comment on materialism.

The house also lays claim to many exclusives: the world's largest fireplace, the greatest collection of animated music-makers and gigantic pipe organs, the world's tallest doll castle, the world's only animated Shaker chimes, the greatest collection of Bauer and Koble stained glass, the largest carousel in history.

Who can tell if it is all true? But then, who cares? It is all too much fun.

Don't miss the carousel. It is a provocative amalgamation, 35 feet tall and 80 feet wide, revolving on 18 wheels with 269 artistic interpretations of real and mythical animals (but no horses), 20,000 lights, and nearly 200 chandeliers.

Another masterpiece is the Mikado music machine, which features two Japanese papier-mâché instrumentalists playing flute and drums, with eyes scanning the crowd, mustaches bobbing, cheeks billowing.

There also are Streets of Yesterday, an entire Main Street of gaslit 19th-century shops and houses scaled down to manageable size; the Cannon Room, with its 50-foot-long, 20-foot-wide guns; the Blue Room, with the "only mechanically operated symphony of its kind in the world." One of the newest additions is the Heritage of the Sea building, housing an entire maritime museum purchased from Seattle, Washington.

At the House on the Rock, Jordan has created his own brave new world of bewilderment: The result is a tour de force—and a *tour de farce*—for the curious visitor.

For More Information

The House on the Rock is open daily, March through October; holiday tours run November through early January. It takes several hours (at least three) for an interested visitor to see everything on self-guided tours. Last tickets are usually sold about two and a half hours before closing, so call ahead to verify last ticket times. Admission is charged.

It is located 40 miles west of Madison on State 23, midway between Spring Green and Dodgeville. For more information, contact House on the Rock, 5754 Highway 23, Spring Green, WI 53588, 608-935-3639.

7

White-Water Rafting

WHITE LAKE

IT WOULD BE A THRILL TO SHOOT THE WILD RAPIDS ON THE mighty Colorado River or to challenge the roiling waters of Idaho's Salmon River as it winds through mountain wilderness. But northern Wisconsin has its own churning maelstrom set to challenge hearty river-rafters: the white-water snarls of the Wolf River, one of the most renowned rapids-infested ribbons in the Midwest.

From early May through June, the Wolf River is usually at its quickest, a snarling, boulder-strewn thread of fast and high white water—thanks to thawing snows and spring rains. Rapids in this stream stretch from one-half to three-quarters of a mile, with average drops of about 25 feet per mile as it runs its rowdy course.

"The great thing about the Wolf is that it is a free-flowing river that rises and falls with changing weather conditions," says Donna Kallner, who (along with husband Bill) operates White Water Specialty in White Lake.

"Every section of the river can vary in temperment daily, depending on recent rains and runoff. So it's rarely the same river twice."

With an international rating that can reach an expert-level class four in spots, springtime white-water rafting on the Wolf demands experience, and its frigid waters may require wet suits. But Kallner notes that rafting, canoeing, or kayaking the Wolf can be done safely if you remember that "white water isn't [an amusement-park ride]; it is nature. The river changes character every few miles, and can go from quiet pools to churning rapids. So play it safe at all times."

That includes using life jackets (sometimes helmets) and learning safety techniques like swimming in rapids and body-ferrying across the river. Kallner teaches such maneuvers during classes at her White Lake outfitting operation.

She cautions that it is probably not a good idea to bring young children onto the turbulent Wolf, especially during high water. "Though the river generally averages two or three feet deep, there are lots of holes in the bed that make it especially dangerous for kids." In fact, several local outfitters have a minimum age requirement (usually 10 or 12 years old) for equipment rental, so check before you go.

Many rafting runs stretch up to 10 miles and take two to six hours to finish the trip. In Langlade County, raft rentals are available at several outfitters along the Wolf.

Wolf River Lodge offers weekend packages with rafts, gear (including life jackets), and transportation, as well as a steak dinner and a private room in a log cabin lodge.

South of White Lake, the Wolf is steeper and more dangerous. It has controlled access on the land of the Menominee Indian Reservation, whose own outfitters can supply rapids-runners with permits and equipment.

In July and August, the river usually mellows considerably, though it boasts some white water through September. Many calm sections become a family haven of summer tubing fun. Just don your swimsuit (and life jacket for kids), float your raft or inner tube atop the calm waters, and hop off for an occasional dip into invigoratingly brisk water.

Trout fishing is another Wolf River summer favorite. Anglers need a Wisconsin inland-waterway trout stamp affixed to their Wisconsin fishing license to ward off aggressive wildlife police and Department of Natural Resources rangers. The river preserves miles of wilderness shoreline that is home to blue heron, eagles, osprey, deer, beaver, and mink.

White Water Specialty, at White Lake, offers all kinds of on the-water classes, including standard one-day canoe and kayak lessons, quiet-water canoe classes, four-day white-water classes, and clinics for families.

FOR MORE INFORMATION

For Wolf River rafting information or a list of outfitters and overnight accommodations, contact Langlade County Chamber of Commerce, P.O. Box 339, Superior Street, Antigo, WI 54409, 715-627-6236; White Water Specialty, N3894 Highway 55, White Lake, WI 54491, 715-882-5400; Wolf River Lodge, Highway 55, White Lake, WI 54491, 715-882-2182.

White-Water Rafting

8

Madtown

MADISON

MADISON IS PROBABLY THE HIPPEST, MOST ECCENTRIC STATE capital in America. It's home to the University of Wisconsin's main campus—often referred to as the Berkeley of the Midwest. Coffee houses, cafés, art galleries, and boutiques line the spoke of streets radiating from the downtown capitol building. Performance artists, musicians, and students transform State Street, a no-cars-allowed thoroughfare running six blocks from the capitol to the university, into an open-air mall filled with surprises. And its scores of ethnic restaurants offer everything from traditional bratwurst sandwiches to Tibetan dumplings.

Way cool, man.

The city, built on a narrow isthmus between Lakes Mendota and Monona (two of Madison's four lakes), revels in its laid-back ambience. Despite the big-town amenities, the big-government institutions, and a giant shadow thrown by one of the largest universities in the country, it's definitely "small-town" friendly and fun. So relax and enjoy.

Start your tour at the Wisconsin State Capitol, located on the isthmus's highest point of land. In good weather, the observation platform in the rotunda dome offers panoramic vistas of water and skyline. On Saturday mornings between April and November, the Capitol Square's 14 acres hosts one of the Midwest's premier farmers markets, selling everything from fresh sweet corn to ice cream made from Wisconsin moo juice.

Then wander down State Street, an eclectic mix of outdoor cafés, coffee houses, clothing stores, and music shops. Serious cappuccino wars are fought along this roadway; one of the most popular spots is Espresso Royale, 650 State Street.

State Street is also home to the Madison Art Center, located inside a beautifully restored movie theater; it features contemporary art, important touring exhibitions, and a great gift store.

Now let's go to school. Not only is UW world-renowned for its academics, but it's been called one of the country's most beautiful campuses. We've got lots of ground to cover; buildings for the college's 42,000 students are spread over nearly 1,000 acres. Tour maps are available at the Visitor Information Place, on Park Street and Observatory Drive, near the Memorial Union.

Since you're nearby, visit the union, especially on warm, sunny days. You can stroll through art exhibits, eat lunch at the Rathskeller, or grab a table on the terrace fronting Lake Mendota, a people-watchers' paradise.

The Geology Museum's skeleton of an American mastodon, which roamed Wisconsin during the Ice Age, is always a crowd pleaser. So are the decorative arts of the Elvehjem Museum, some dating back to 2300 B.C. And the view from Bascom Hill offers the city's best glimpses of the state capitol. (Local lore says the hill's seated statue of Abe Lincoln stands when a virgin passes by. I've never seen Abe stretch to his full height yet.)

If you can't get out of your car for a look around, take Observatory Drive for "the prettiest ride through campus." It winds through woodlands to Washburn Observatory, open to the public (in clear weather) on the first and third Wednesday nights of every month.

During football season, Bucky Badger leads Wisconsin's warriors into Big Ten conference battles with the likes of Illinois and Michigan at Camp Randall Stadium. He also oversees a "fifth quarter" at games' end, allowing the UW marching band a chance to strut their acclaimed stuff, including oom-pah tunes and polkas. If you're in the stands, you'll actually feel the bleachers shake, rattle, and roll.

No visit to UW would be complete without a stop at Babcock Hall; the food-sciences building features its own dairy store—and maybe the most delicious ice cream on any college campus. Come late afternoons to see the university's dairy herd being milked.

Back in town, another must-visit is the Canterbury Booksellers Coffeehouse, 315 Gorham Street. Not only does it offer hundreds of hard-to-find titles and reading areas with comfy couches and Oriental rugs, but almost nightly performances on its stage boast everything from author's readings and performance art to live music and kids' storytelling.

Food is the last item on this Madison touring menu. These are two highlights suggested by a Madison-native friend of mine (and a former top honcho with the state's Division of Tourism): Ella's Deli & Ice Cream Parlor (2902 East Washington Street) is a city institution, serving kosher-style sandwiches and huge sundaes, but its most unusual lure is a vintage 1927 carousel that anyone can ride for less than a buck. For authentic college-town flavor, the Wild Iris Café (1255 Regent Street) is crowded, funky, and famed for its Mediterranean meals.

Madtown

FOR MORE INFORMATION

For more Madison information, contact Greater Madison Convention & Visitors Bureau, 615 East Washington Street, Madison, WI 53703, 800-373-6376 or 608-255-2537.

9

Honey Acres

ASHIPPUN

NESTLED IN THE "BEE-UTIFUL" HILLS OF SOUTHEASTERN WIS-
consin is a sweet little museum promising a honey of a
good time that'll have you buzzing about the fun long
after you leave. So pack up the family and swarm to Honey
Acres, located near Ashippun, about 12 miles north of
Oconomowoc.

Owned by the Diehnelts, beekeepers and honey packers
here since 1852, Honey Acres tells the story of bee society,
honey making, and beekeeping from the earliest days of
Egyptian pharaohs to modern times. It also offers close-up
views of bee activities in a hollowed "bee tree." You'll sample five kinds of honey at the end of your self-guided tour.
And you'll learn interesting factoids about bees and the
honey-making process that will amaze and dazzle friends,
such as:

- Bees have four wings.
- An average worker bee visits 50 to 100 flowers on each
  collection trip.
- They must travel 25,000 miles to produce one pound of
  honey—that's equidistant to one time around the world.
- In order to keep hives "air-conditioned," certain bees are

appointed the job of flapping their wings (250 times per second) to provide cooling breezes.
- Which state is nicknamed the "Beehive State"? (Answer at the end of story.)

Honey Acres started almost 150 years ago when Christian Diehnelt brought his beekeeping skills to these Wisconsin meadowlands from his native Rosswein, Germany. Unbroken fields of fresh clover and wildflowers, perfect conditions for an apiary, took the sting out of starting a new business in pioneer times.

Today, fifth-generation master beekeeper Walter J. Diehnelt oversees 1,800 bee hives (with more than 50,000 bees in each box) that produce nearly 150,000 pounds of honey annually.

Start out at the museum's small theater for a 20-minute film that explains everything you want to know about bees, honey, and beekeeping. (I dare you not to cringe during a *close-up* shot of a bee stinging a person's finger.) Then take a walk through the museum exhibits, which reveal some fascinating honey history.

For example, one display tells that honey pots were found in King Tut's tomb. Seems Egyptians of 4,500 years ago used honey as medicine, for religious rites, and, most importantly, in tombs as food for the afterlife. Apparently, they took that postmortem snack seriously: more than 15 tons of honey were found in the burial chambers of Ramses III.

Another section reveals that colonists first brought honeybees to Virginia in 1620. Called "White Man's Fly" by Native Americans, it's said that when Indians saw these bees swarm and move westward, they knew the White Man would soon follow.

You'll also learn about beekeeping around the world. Panama seems like the best place to produce honey, since beekeepers there use stingless bees. Clay pots are preferred instead of wooden boxes, or hives, in Lebanon and Israel. Yugoslavia should get an award for its beehive "cabinets"— armoirelike pieces handpainted with colorful folk art murals that "help bees return to the correct hive."

A favorite among kids is the bee tree, where you can observe thousands of swarming bees in action inside their log hive while standing safely behind a glass partition. It still gives me the creeps, having been stung three times in the span of a month by rowdy cousins of these sometimes pesky insects.

The tasting room ends your indoor tour. Here you'll learn that the color and flavor of honey depends on the kind of blossoms visited by honeybees. In fact, colors range from water white to dark amber; flavors, from mild to bold.

I found the wildflower honey sweet and pure. Daughters Kate and Dayne flipped for light clover honey. My father liked the hearty buckwheat. Mom, an indiscriminate honey lover, enjoyed them all. We couldn't leave without buying some of everything to take home.

Before you leave Honey Acres, follow the museum's nature trail (about a 10-minute round-trip) to see three antique bee boxes and get a panoramic vista of the surrounding valleys.

Oh yes. The "Beehive State" is—Utah.

FOR MORE INFORMATION

Allow about one hour for your visit. Admission is free. Open all year, except holidays, Honey Acres is located two miles north of Ashippun on State 67, 12 miles north of I-94 (Oconomowoc exit). For more information, contact Honey Acres, Highway 67, Ashippun, WI 53003, 920-474-4411.

10

Pendarvis

MINERAL POINT

LOOK INTO THE SURROUNDING HILLS AND YOU'LL SEE "BADGER holes," cavelike gaps burrowed into hillsides by miners in search of rich lead and zinc deposits that transformed the tiny village of Mineral Point into an 1830s boomtown.

The miners, mostly from southern Illinois and Missouri, lived in these holes during mild weather, returning home during the cold season. They were a rough lot, working all day and drinking all night, constantly brawling over jumped claims.

But it took a hardy breed of men from Cornwall, England, to bring peace to the region. The Cornish brought their families to Mineral Point in 1841; built the first permanent homes, churches, and schools in the area; and left a legacy of their hard work and skills that we still can enjoy today.

That's especially true at Pendarvis, a Wisconsin state historic site that includes six restored 1840s miner's cottages located on their original sites. The houses are built of local limestone and fashioned to resemble homes left behind in England. However, they are very dark and gloomy inside, with low ceilings. Many built their homes at the bottom of ravines. Some even burrowed into the sides of hills. (This area became known as Shake-Rag-Under-the-Hill, from the custom of women summoning their husbands by waving a white rag from their doorways. The rags could be seen from mines across the ravine.)

You can judge for yourself just how dark and gloomy these homes really are during tours of the houses. Occasionally, Pendarvis also offers candlelight tours led by costumed interpreters. During annual festivals, there often will be people on the grounds demonstrating candlemaking, preparing food, and performing other typical 1840s chores. Especially interesting is a three-story limestone and log house built into the side of a cliff, with its root cellar jutting into the hillside.

After touring the homes, wander across the street to Pendarvis's 43-acre "mining grounds," where you can take a self-guided tour of crude "badger holes" and other mining legacies. Most famous is Merry Christmas Mine Hill, so named because lead ore was discovered there on Christmas Day.

Several area restaurants serve typical mining-era Cornish foods. Try the pasties, a meat-and-potato pie that was the 1840s equivalent of a fast-food hamburger. Overnighters might want to stay in an authentic Cornish building; try the Chesterfield Inn, originally an 1834 stagecoach stop. It has foot-thick walls, low ceilings, and narrow doorways, but its eight charming guest rooms have been completely restored with period antiques. The inn also boasts a good restaurant.

Finally, head down to Shake Rag Alley, the oldest arts and crafts area in Mineral Point. Clustered around the old Federal Spring watering hole, artisans demonstrate 19th-century crafts inside dwellings built by early settlers.

If you visit Pendarvis during one of its annual weekend festivals, you can double your fun. These celebrations include Flavours of Old Cornwall, on the last weekend in

June, when costumed guides prepare pioneer Cornish favorites like pasties, saffron cake, and clotted cream; Drolls of Old Cornwall, on two Saturdays in mid-July and two in early August, when storytellers spin "drolls" (Cornish folktales) in the Kiddleywink Pub; and Sun, Moon, and Stars, mid-September, featuring antique quilts, coverlets, and other textile handicrafts displayed in historic surroundings.

FOR MORE INFORMATION

Pendarvis is open May through October; there is a small charge for guided tours. For more information, contact the settlement at 114 Shake Rag Street, Mineral Point, WI 53565, 608-987-2122, or contact the Chamber of Commerce, 237 High Street, P.O. Box 78, Mineral Point, WI 53565, 608-987-3201.

Pendarvis

11

Fantasy Getaway Suites

RELATIONSHIP EXPERTS SUGGEST THAT COUPLES SHOULD BUD-
get some time just for themselves. You know, pack up the
kids to bring to Grandma's, leave the dog with a neighbor,
and point the car toward some romantic destination that'll
add some excitement to the monotony of work and personal
responsibilities.

If you're going to follow their advice, why opt for a regular room at a fancy downtown hotel when you can experience adventures you may have only dreamed of?. Wisconsin
provides some unusual and eccentric getaways that could
add sparks to your romantic engines.

Wild imaginations help at the West Bend FantaSuite Hotel
in West Bend, which offers 25 specialty rooms. Consider the
Odyssey, which resembles a Gemini space capsule, complete
with a 10-sided waterbed, TV, video games, stereo, elaborate
"control board," multicolored rotating lights, and a romantic "moon crater" whirlpool surrounded by a rocky lunar
landscape.

It's enough to make Mr. Spock's pointy ears turn red.

Or mush to Northern Lights, which is shaped like an igloo
with blocks of "ice" walls and a light system that simulates
the shimmering aurora borealis.

It takes more than $100,000 to outfit each specialty suite.

But if you're undecided about which fantasy you fancy, take a peek at the front desk's portfolio which offers color photos of all rooms. Or visit any Sunday for free 2:00 P.M. tours; note that crowds sometimes number 200 or more.

Maybe you'll discover that you'd rather sack on a rack. The Dungeon suite features a giant (make-believe) torture rack as the bed, perfect for stretching out. Le Cave, which resembles an underground cave, reminds me of Fred Flintstone's digs. Cupid's Corner is the Poconos gone wild, with heart-shaped waterbed and mirrored ceilings. And in the Wild Wild West, you sleep in a covered wagon and bathe in a horse-trough-shaped whirlpool.

But my favorite is The Continental, built to resemble a 1960s drive-in. The "parked" 1964 Lincoln Continental comes with a clip-on snack tray, car speaker, and big-screen TV that doubles as the movie screen. The bed? Yep, it's in the car's back seat.

Train aficionados should choo-choo to the End of the Line, a Lake Geneva caboose hotel where 43 Chicago & North Western and Milwaukee Road cabooses line the property. And *line* is certainly the right description.

The "motel" is situated on the old railroad bed right-of-way leading into town. So the property is only 100 feet wide, with cabooses strung out for more than a third of a mile.

Twenty-five cabooses have modern berths—fully carpeted with double bed, sofa, and bathroom with shower; some offer skylights in the caboose cupola. End of the Line also offers two suites in a converted Chicago & North Western Pullman car. The Rockefeller Suite is pure art deco, sleek lines and subtle colors; the Victorian Suite drips red and gold velvet. One- and two-bedroom caboose villas are the newest additions.

The Don Q Inn has always been a little unusual. You'll probably agree after seeing the Dodgeville hostelry's unique lawn ornament—a massive Boeing C-97, the last of the gasoline-powered prop-jobs, plunked in the front yard. It also has an underground tunnel connecting the motel and restaurant, and for at least a dozen years it has offered fantasy suites with "caveman" and "Tarzan" motifs.

But the ultimate overnight here is the Church Steeple. Couples climb stairs to reach a door cut into a genuine three-story church steeple, complete with bell tower. Inside the spire, they revel in heavenly but rustic surroundings that include a 300-gallon copper-tub whirlpool on the first floor, Victorian bedroom on the second floor, and a third-floor sitting room completely furnished with throw pillows. All levels have television; cocktails the evening of arrival and a continental breakfast the following day are a part of the pampering package.

FOR MORE INFORMATION

West Bend FantaSuite Hotel, 2520 West Washington Street, West Bend, WI 53095, 800-727-9727. Rates include champagne and continental breakfast in bed (or full breakfast in the restaurant). End of the Line Vacation Station, 301 East Town Line Road, Lake Geneva, WI 53147, 414-248-7245; Don Q Inn, Box 199, Dodgeville, WI 53533, 608-935-2321.

Fantasy Getaway Suites

12

An Artisan Adventure

CAMBRIDGE

RECENTLY A FRIEND CALLED UP AND ASKED IF I'D EVER BEEN TO Cambridge. Well, heck, I'm a Big Shot Travel Writer. I've been all around the world. Of course I'd been to Cambridge, and Oxford, and . . .

"No, no," he interrupted. "Cambridge, Wisconsin."

"Huh?"

I didn't even know where to find this little village on the map. And even when my buddy told me that Cambridge rests about 20 minutes southeast of Madison, Mr. Big Shot Travel Writer still couldn't find it on the map.

But it turns out that Cambridge is worth looking for. In fact, the town quickly became one of my favorite travel-destination discoveries in the last five years.

It's not surprising, either. Not only has this thriving artistic community, crammed with talented artisans and their shops, been voted the most friendly small town by *Wisconsin Trails* magazine; it also has a Chicago connection.

Paul and Andrea Miller run Cambridge's Music and Memories, a browser's delight that sells everything from very affordable to very exotic music boxes. For years Andrea, a native Chicago South Sider, operated music stores in the Chicago area, with showcase shops in downtown Water

Tower Place and in suburban Northbrook Court, Randhurst Mall, and Prospect Mall.

When she and husband, Paul, who's originally from Michigan, decided it was time in 1992 to leave Chicago and look for a quieter place to live, they stumbled upon Cambridge.

"It had a certain charm to it," Andrea says, "a quiet little place with lots of artists and interesting people."

The Millers opened up Music and Memories about five years ago, occupying two small rooms on a corner building in the center of "downtown" Mill Street. Today it's a sprawling paradise of music boxes from around the world, with "quite a Chicago following," Andrea adds.

Cambridge has blossomed, too. New specialty stores feature everything from Amish handiwork and Native American art to South American folk art and pottery galore. "It's the kind of place that people like to escape to for the weekend," comments Andrea.

That's just what my family did a few weeks ago when we visited this artsy hamlet. And Music and Memories was a highlight on my "must-see" list for several reasons. Mainly, I have been looking for a special music box for my Irish mother for nearly 10 years—one that plays "An Irish Lullaby," a song that my mom used to sing to me nearly every night as I fell asleep as a little kid.

Paul and Andrea first showed me around the store. It's quite fascinating to see all the different kinds of music boxes here—more than 2,000 of them on display, playing about 700 different songs.

The cheapest costs $11; it's in the shape of a tiny gift bag with "music" in it. The mose expensive runs about $13,000; handmade by a Vermont artisan, it plays huge discs (with 1,000 different songs available) and is housed in a box of inlaid Italian wood.

"We actually sell one almost every year," Paul says.

Paul, who was a computer-operations systems analyst prior to Music and Memories, has taken on the craft of a dying breed—music box tuner and expert repairman. An art form in itself making extensive repairs may take about six months, working on about four music boxes at a time. That's because it's an exacting job, requiring a gemcutter's eye and a musician's ear. In fact, Paul says there are only about 20 to 25 full-time music-box experts in the United States.

Most novelty music boxes are pretty simple, maxing out at about 18 notes. More complicated are 36-note boxes that also can play chords. Then there are the 72-note classics, most difficult to return to their original tympany, which might include bells, note and chord runs, and chimes. By the way, the best woods are rosewood and walnut because of their resonant qualities.

A great way to learn more about the world of music boxes is to have Paul and Andrea take you on a tour of their store. You'll see all kinds of fascinating collector contraptions—chirping bird boxes that run from $850 ro $1,000; late 1700s-style cylinder boxes in the shape of a mosque that go for $585; and even musical snuff boxes that sell for $1,800 to $2,500.

There also are plenty of cute and affordable music boxes for you and me.

And yes, Paul and Andrea were able to find me that "Irish Lullaby" music box I'd been looking for during the past decade. Don't tell Mom—it's a Christmas present!

Cambridge has another Illinois connection—the Wells Clay Works. We stumbled upon Brad Wells's simple, elegant pottery while browsing the town. He was repairing a shelf in the back of his gallery when my daughters became fascinated by his dog, a German Shepherd named Karma. We started to talk, he offered to "throw a pot" for us down in

An Artisan Adventure

his 1,200-square foot workshop, and the fascination never stopped.

Wells creates his pottery while standing, "like the old Southern potters did," he said. The artisan has been creating elegant, functional pottery for more than 20 years, beginning with an apprenticeship at age 15.

He's already accomplished quite a bit in his field. His resume includes a studio assistantship at the Kansas City Art Institute, one of the country's premier centers for study of the ceramic arts; a line of contemporary redware featured at Pleasant Hill, a Shaker Village and national historic site in Kentucky; and stoneware for the Galena Pottery Company of Illinois based on earthenware produced in 19th-century Galena.

But it's the aesthetically pleasing and functional simplicity of his work that got to my soul—what he calls a combination of the simplicity of early American pottery and the quiet elegance of oriental porcelain, with rich matte glazes of the Arts and Crafts period.

"I like to create pottery that is accessible," Wells explained as he threw a pot on his wheel. "I don't want somebody to buy one of my pieces and then just put it up on a shelf and look at it. I want them to use it. I want it to become part of their daily life. That's what I find rewarding."

It's incredibly affordable, too. We returned home with an armful of Wells pottery—which we use. Every day.

Finally, don't pass up an opportunity during your visit to eat at the Clay Market Café, located in the heart of "downtown." Great food, and it's eclectic. The hip menu includes everything from Pork Tenderloin Benedict for breakfast or chicken and roma tomatoes in pesto sauce for lunch to dinner's roasted garlic, ricotta cheese-filled spinach ravioli.

And they use Wells's pottery here, too.

For More Information

Cambridge is about two hours north of Chicago, off Interstate 90 to Highway 73 North, then to Highway B east; you'll arrive in Cambridge at the Village Square. For more information, call 608-423-3780. The town also has its own website: http://www.bminet.com/cambridge.

An Artisan Adventure

Summer

13

Wisconsin Dells Family Fling

WATER PARKS, BEST HOTELS, COOLEST ATTRACTIONS

Water Parks

Wisconsin Dells water parks are so hot, they're cool, getting "wave reviews" from summer funseekers.

Everybody from families with little tykes who like to splash, slip, and slide in knee-high water to dedicated water rats who ride ocean-size breakers or surfboards has enjoyed these wet and wild havens while looking for soak-filled thrills.

The Dells boasts three huge water parks, complete with slides, floating islands, and other splashy gizmos; make that four, if you include a fabulous motel with so much water fun that it should qualify as a kind of water park, too. So here's a guide to the Dells' water parks, compiled by the slightly waterlogged Puhala family, which includes my wife, Debbie, and daughters Kate and Dayne at ages eight and six.

Noah's Ark is "America's largest water park," sprawling over 65 acres in the water-park capital of the Midwest. It's so big that 4 million gallons of water are used to propel 45 different water activities. You can cannonball down 25 water slides, ride breakers in the Midwest's two largest wave pools, or float down the region's two longest lazy rivers. Plan to spend the entire day; you'll never want to leave.

The "Big Kahuna" wave pool is one of the largest in the country, generating surfing-size waves. Families with smaller kids might opt for "The Wave"; a corner of this pool features "Swirl River," a children's section surrounded by "breakwater lanes" that soften wave action, allowing little kids to join in the fun while splashing in an area no deeper than three feet.

We bit the bullet and stood in a 45-minute line to ride "Congo Bongo Rapids," a $1 million attraction that allows five people to sit in eight-foot-wide inner tubes and plunge down a 700-foot water slide. We also headed to "Slide-winders," where the kids could scamper down one of five different slides (from gentle to adventurous) with virtually no wait.

Serious thrillseekers shouldn't miss "Paradise Lagoon," with its Tarzan cable drops that unceremoniously toss you into water 11 feet deep. Super-fast Cannonball slides get a bang out of riders. And see if you can make it across tricky "Lily Pad Walks" without getting dumped in the drink.

Others make a beeline for "The Plunge," a sheer 45-foot drop at double speed. I dare you not to scream on the way down. Or try the park's scary plunge "Black Thunder," where you barrel down a pitch-black chute to churning water below or the "Dark Voyage" which has more of the same but for the entire family at once, in a giant inner tube.

Toddlers love the park's four kiddie and soft-play (foam-padded) water areas. They can run under sprinkling mushrooms, swing, and slide. Tykes can even take aim with squirt guns.

To all this add a "Water Animal Extravaganza" (cartoon characters singing and dancing), daily at each wave pool. There is live music at the "River Rat Saloon" (heavy on the Jimmy Buffet and Jim Croce); 3,500 lounge chairs (all taken unless you get there early); the best surf shops in the Midwest (offering more than 5,000 swimsuits from lines like Gotcha, Body Glove, and Billabong); bumper boats and go-carts; minigolf; and much more.

Noah's Ark is located on the strip along Wisconsin 12. It's open daily through September 7 and offers all-day unlimited passes. Call 608-254-6351.

Family Land, the Dells' second largest water park, offers lots of high-speed thrills. "Demon's Drop," the "world's steepest and fastest water slide," is an 85-foot sheer drop down a blue flume into a pool of water; it feels like you're dropping off the end of the earth.

Debbie zoomed down "Double Rampage," the Dells' only hydroplane sleds, that had her climbing up to a four-story tower, then sledding down the ramp, and skimming across the water at supersonic speed while she whooped loud enough to curdle cows' milk in the next county.

Another favorite is "Blue Magnum," a 2,000-foot-long super flume full of twists, turns, and tunnels with names like "Wipe Out," "Kamikaze," and "Corkscrew." Then there's "Dragon's Tail," a seven-story, double-drop speed slide that we could never master. Let's not forget the "Tidal Wave," a 950,000-gallon pool that had Kate and me riding five-foot waves on our inner tube.

There's plenty for little kids, too. The "Fountain of Youth" playground features a Dumbo slide and spraying mushrooms. And there are lots of "U-drive-'em" amusement-park rides including bumper boats, bumper cars, and roller coasters.

Family Land is located on U.S. 12. It's open daily through September 7. Admission includes unlimited rides. Call 608-254-7766.

Riverview Park and Waterworld boasts the Dells' "largest kids' water and ride playground." In fact, the park has expanded to twice its former size in the past two years.

Children rule at "Kid's Kingdom." Kate and Dayne climbed aboard a dragon roller coaster, bumper boats, and go-carts; tested their flying skills on airplane and helicopter rides; and got a panoramic view of the park on the Sky Ride (similar to a ski lift). Other rides include a carousel, train, kiddie Indy racers, tilt-a-whirl, high-speed scramblers, and more.

A beefed-up water activity area has several new additions: "Wild Island," built especially for kids, offers chute-slides, water slides, and 28 ways to control water flowing through a network of valves. Then there's "The Beach," an ocean-wave pool; "Flash Flood," a superspeed water slide propelled by a column of rushing water; and the "Hydro Spa," a 30-person whirlpool that offers great vistas of the water park below.

There's also an activity pool for "kids" of all ages, where you can mow down swimmers with water cannons, test your balance on the log walk and lily pads, and slip and slide on "Giant Snake" and "Gator Alley."

Riverview Park is located on U.S. 12. It's open daily through September 7; admission includes unlimited rides. Call 608-254-2608.

Sure, the Polynesian is a hotel. But with its new hands-on interactive kiddie pool adding to three other water activity areas, it's more like a water park with a room. It's easily the best place to overnight in the Dells if you have kids 12 and under who want nonstop water wriggling.

Kids flock to the hotel's new kiddie pool. It resembles a giant "Lego-land" with swinging ropes, tire swings, tube slide, geysers, and a treetop house featuring scores of handles, wheels, pull ropes, and buttons that send water spraying in all directions. The pool area is only 18 inches deep, so parents can relax while their kids frolic, and the slide landing areas are padded with foam.

Summer

Dayne loved another kid pool that resembles a rocky mountain lagoon, complete with waterfall and water slide emptying into three and a half feet of water. Yet another kiddie water-activity area offers swings, spraying mushrooms, and a gentle "whale" water slide. Bigger kids can swim on the other side of the waterfall or try another pool area outfitted with a volleyball net.

Several of the hotel's 230 rooms have patio doors opening right onto the pool area. Others have balconies overlooking all water activities. Accommodations range from budget rooms to luxurious three-room suites.

Come during the winter and enjoy what I call "Indoor Florida," the hotel's two huge indoor pools that include floating "animal islands," water slides, and a hands-on water-activity area that boasts everything from shooting sprays and water geysers to tipping buckets and water guns. Call 608-254-2883.

Best Hotels

Since it first opened I'd heard the buzz—there's a hot new resort hotel up in the Dells that blows all the others out of the water. But I figured that was just more hype.

I was wrong.

After spending a long weekend with my family at Black Wolf Lodge, I can say unequivocally that all the other hotels in the Midwest's No. 1 family-vacation destination have their work cut out for them: now they're going to be judged by a whole new standard. And matching or beating the elegant and gracious Black Wolf Lodge is going to be really difficult.

Just from the outside, it's a winner. Its huge "log" lodge construction (230,000 square feet) of western red cedar, nestled on 35 scenic acres, reminds me of those great western national park lodges, such as the one at Yellowstone.

So you already know the 206-room Black Wolf is something special even before you set foot inside a lobby that simply overwhelms visitors and sets the tone for their stay with its three-story stone fireplace, vaulted cathedral ceiling, massive antler chandeliers, handmade and over-sized log furniture, and taxidermied Up North creatures to satisfy any Great White North cravings. (Kids, note that the namesake "Black Wolf" resides just above the registration desk.)

Just about everything inside the Black Wolf is handcrafted by artisans from 10 different states. The lodge's owners sought out Amish and Mennonite communities in Michigan, who joined Wisconsin artisans in producing everything from handsome hickory chairs to log and timbered furniture. Western-style decorative rugs and wall hangings were loomed in Mexico; the large elk and moose chandeliers in the lobby were created by an artisan from northern Wisconsin; and even the lobby's white-cedar, oversized chairs and sofas were handmade by two brother in Idaho.

Still more superlatives are needed. Its Spirit Island boasts the "nation's largest indoor water facility," with more than 20,000 square feet of splish-splashy fun—waterslides, waterfalls, bubbling geysers, whirlpools—as well as the "world's longest" indoor lazy river.

If you'd rather hit the sunshine, what better source for outdoor water fun than challenging the two four-story, 450-foot semi-enclosed inner-tube waterslides. Or try your hand at a game of water basketball and see if you're another "Splash" Jordan.

Yep, staying at Black Wolf is like having your own personal water park.

And there are so many extras. Exquisite guest rooms come in seven different styles. We stayed in a suite boasting a loft sleeping area (perfect for kids who don't want to be in parents' eye-view 24 hours per day), gas fireplace, cathedral ceiling, and private balcony. Some rooms have big-screen TVs (with Nintendo and pay-TV movies) and whirlpools. All have microwaves and refrigerators.

There's also an arcade to end all arcade rooms: 70 games that spit out redemption coupons kids can cash in for prizes. And a really important note for families with kids in tow—Black Wolf's thin-crusted pizza, served at the Loose Moose Lounge, is scrumptious.

Of course, while Black Wolf is running the table with its word-of-mouth buzz, other Dells resort hotels are attempting to meet the challenge. In a heartbeat I'd stay at the Wilderness Resort, which still has the most spectacular outdoor pool in the Dells, especially now that it's added the Gold Rush Tube Slide, which whooshes riders more than 400 feet off a 40-foot-tall tower. It also boasts Prospector's Creek, a 600-foot lazy river, perfect for hot, sunny afternoons.

The Polynesian Resort Hotel is another premier water wonderland, offering everything from 300-foot water slides to a 500-foot outdoor lazy river. And with all its kids' water playlands (including an outdoor, interactive pirate ship and a huge indoor "water factory" with even more splashy gadgets), the Polynesian may still be the best place to stay for families with kids under 10 years of age.

But there's something about Black Wolf that really captures the imagination and takes you away from your everyday worries. Maybe it's all the north woodsy stuff. Maybe its the gracious elegance, somewhat unexpected in the Dells. Whatever, isn't that what a vacation is all about?

Room rates range from $83 to $259, depending on the season; there's a two-night minimum for July and August weekends. For more information, call 800-559-9653 or 608-253-2222.

Coolest Attractions

Okay, there's more. Sure, you're staying at a great hotel. But you've got to get out and work the Dells for even more family fun. And unless you have a suitcase full of money, you'll need to know which attractions will give you the biggest bang for your buck. No problem.

Following are some of my favorites:

- Even if your hotel has a great water-park, spend a day at Noah's Ark, the nation's largest outdoor water-park, which celebrated its 20th summer in 1998. Having the Big Kahuna wave pool; "Dark Voyage" and "Black Thunder" (the Midwest's only dark tunnel waterslides), adventure rivers, kiddie pools, and family tube rides—this place rocks! Call 608-254-6351.

- The Tommy Bartlett Thrill Show just keeps on getting better. Besides water-ski pyramids and daredevil maneuvers, the aerialist who walks atop a spinning 65-foot-pendulum wheel makes you're heart flutter. And juggler-comedian Dieter Tasso always breaks me up. Call 608-254-2525.

- In a town that's go-cart crazy, I'll put my money on King Ludwig's Adventure Park, where you can race over hairpin turns and do figure eights on wooden tracks in everything from standard go-carts to winged "Kart-style" race cars and NASCAR look-alikes. Call 608-254-5464.

- The Crystal Grand Theater brings a bit of Branson-style entertainment to the Dells. Big names slated for shows in 1998, for example, included Randy Travis and Bill Cosby. Call 608-254-4545.

- Thunder Valley Inn serves the best breakfast in south-central Wisconsin. This historic Norwegian farmstead is run by Anita, Sigrid, and Kari Nelson, who welcome you like part of the family. They boast goodies like Swedish pancakes with lingonberries and the biggest (and most delicious) cinnamon rolls in the world; the family might even regale you with a Norwegian fiddle tune or mountain ballad. They operate a bed and breakfast here, too. This is a "can't miss" during your Dells visit. Call 608-254-4145.

- Did I mention that Tommy Bartlett's Robot World & Exploratory has the original Russian space station, *mir*, on display? It's one of only three in the world—one's in a Russian warehouse and the other just came back from orbiting the earth. How'd they do that? Call 608-254-2525.

- I'd go down the Timber Wolf Log Ride a million times more; it passes through dark caves, under thundering waterfalls, and circles an "active volcano" that erupts every 15 minutes. Call 608-254-8414.

- An eight-and-a-half-mile tour on World War II amphibious "ducks" is still a treat. The lumbering vehicles ply backwoods trails and plunge into the Wisconsin River, Dell Creek, and Lake Delton. Call 608-254-8751.

Finally, the Dells have been invaded by thrill rides. And, believe me, size matters! King Ludwig offers the most stomach-turning contraption, a 160-foot-tall device called the Skyscraper that's simply two revolving seats attached to each end of this massive armlike structure making giant circles in the air. Don't eat pizza before this one. Call 608-254-5464.

Air Boingo boasts a Bungee Jump, Bungee Trampoline, Ejection Seat, and the Space Shot, which drops you down with the G-force of a suborbital flight. Call 608-253-5867.

And Big Chief Go-Kart has three wooden roller coasters: Zeus (the wildest ride), Pegasus (for kids), and Cyclops (a 'tweener). It also offers a go-cart track that goes through the belly of a giant Trojan Horse. Go figure. Call 608-254-2490.

For More Information

For mailing addresses and other Dells information, contact Wisconsin Dells Visitors & Convention Bureau, 701 Superior Street, P.O. Box 390, Wisconsin Dells, WI 53965, 800-223-3557 or 608-254-8088.

14

Wright Stuff Tours

WISCONSIN HAS PLENTY OF THE WRIGHT STUFF.

Frank Lloyd Wright, one of America's premier architects, was born in 1867 in Richland Center. His 600-acre estate still stands in Spring Green. And more than 40 Wright-designed buildings, most of them private homes, can be found within Wisconsin's borders.

Most of Wright's buildings, though revered as architectural icons, continue to be used as intended: homes are still homes; office buildings remain office buildings; restaurants continue to be restaurants; churches still welcome worshippers. That is fitting for the works of a man who once said, "A building is not just a place to be. It is a way to be."

While there are no formal Wright tours that travel statewide to his creations, weekenders can fashion their own "Wright heritage tour," rambling across Wisconsin's landscape to seven of the most impressive Wright sites that encompass his 70-year career. Here are some highlights:

Albert Dell German Warehouse Located in Richland Center, 30 miles northwest of Spring Green, the Albert Dell German Warehouse is one of Wright's early designs. The four-story, red-brick building, constructed between 1917 and 1921, is noted for its elaborate geometrically shaped cast-concrete friezes. There's a theater on the first floor, with photos and murals illustrating his work on the second floor. Guided tours, by reservation only, are conducted May through November for four dollars per person. Call 608-647-2808.

Richland Center also hosts the Frank Lloyd Wright Birthday Celebration in early June. Warehouse tours, Wright lectures, architectural displays, trolley rides, and food stands are part of the program. For festival information, call 608-647-6205.

Taliesin One of Wright's most famous creations, Taliesin is his 600-acre estate in Spring Green. Built in 1911, it stands sentinel at the edge of a hill 60-plus feet above the Wisconsin River valley. Here at his home, office, and studio of some 50 years, visitors can get the most personal glimpse of the legendary architect.

From June through September guided morning walking tours (operated Mondays through Saturdays) wind more than two miles past Wright's Hillside Home School, the Romeo and Juliet Windmill Tower, and the Midway Farm. You'll also visit Taliesin's formal gardens. Admission is charged.

From mid-June through September you can take a three-hour tour of the house itself, which first opened for public inspection in 1991. Especially dramatic is Wright's living room, all vertical and horizontal space flooded with light from banks of windows overlooking the valley and water gardens below.

The house tour includes refreshments in the Taliesin outdoor tea circle, where Wright often entertained guests and apprentices. There are two afternoon tours, Thursdays through Saturdays; admission is charged. For information, call 608-588-7948.

Hillside Home School at Taliesin Designed by Wright in 1902, the Hillside Home School is where you can see architects and apprentices taking part in the Frank Lloyd Wright School of Architecture's experimental education program. Especially impressive is a huge drafting studio, likened by Wright to "an abstract forest with light pouring in from the ceiling." There's also a small theater, gift shop, and galleries containing Wright-designed furniture and photo murals. Daily hourly tours are conducted May through October; admission is charged. Call 608-588-2511.

Seth Peterson Cottage Located in Lake Delton, Seth Peterson Cottage is a 1958 Wright design that can be rented for a weekend stay. The cottage is balanced on the edge of a secluded ridge that plunges down to Mirror Lake in one of the most popular state parks near Wisconsin Dells.

Though only 900 square feet, the cottage feels big architecturally, with a soaring roof that has no visible means of support, panoramic views of the lake and forest, and a huge fireplace of horizontally layered local sandstone.

Year-round tours, by reservation only, are conducted on the second Sunday of each month; admission is charged. For tour or rental information, call 608-254-6051 or 608-254-6551.

Unitarian Meetinghouse Designed by Wright in 1946, the Unitarian Meetinghouse stands in Madison, 40 miles east of Spring Green. The meetinghouse, at 900 University Bay Drive, is constructed of native limestone, copper, and glass. Members of the congregation hauled tons of stones for the church's thick walls from a nearby quarry to the site and helped finish the interior. Visitors can attend summer Sunday morning services at 10 A.M. Guided tours (admission is charged) are available May through September, Tuesdays through Saturdays. Call 608-233-9774.

Annunciation Greek Orthodox Church Located in Milwaukee, the Annunciation Greek Orthodox Church is another Wright house of worship. Designed in 1956 as one of the architect's last major commissions, the circular building at 9400 West Congress is vastly different from traditional Byzantine architecture.

Its domed shape resembles the spacecraft from the movie *Close Encounters of the Third Kind*. The building also boasts gold icon screens and sunken gardens. Visitors are welcome to attend liturgy services at 10 A.M. on Sundays. Year-round tours, by reservation only, are given Monday through Friday; admission is charged. Call 414-461-9400.

S.C. Johnson Wax Administration Center Located in Racine, the S.C. Johnson Wax Administration Center has been a mecca for architects, Wright devotees, and tourists from around the world since it opened in 1939. The futuristic design, astounding even today, speaks eloquently to one of Wright's dictums: "If you make men and women proud of their environment and happy to be where they are, it all comes out to the good where the product is concerned."

Especially noteworthy is the Great Workroom, main office area for the company's international headquarters. It covers nearly a half-acre, with slim columns (resembling huge golf tees) supporting the roof and almost 50 miles of glass tubing replacing conventional windows. Even the Cherokee-red bricks are unusual—more than 200 sizes and shapes made to form the building's many angles and curves.

Guided tours are offered Tuesdays through Fridays year-round, and on weekends from Memorial Day through Labor

Day. Admission is free, but reservations are required; call
414-260-2154.

For More Information

For more Wright information, contact Spring Green Chamber of Commerce, P.O. Box 3, Spring Green, WI 53588, 608-588-2042.

Wright Stuff Tours

15

Bayfield and the Apostle Islands

BAYFIELD

IF YOU VISIT BAYFIELD, A HISTORIC FISHING VILLAGE LOCATED on the southwestern shores of Lake Superior, you'll no doubt also spend some time in the Apostle Islands, one of the state's premier natural treasures. The town is one that time has largely forgotten, offering a looking-glass glimpse of the past that lingers in fisheries, docks, and historic architecture. The 21-island archipelago and its miles of unspoiled shoreline are filled with the lore of Indians, French fur traders, and the mysteries of the sea.

Bayfield

Bayfield's hopes of being transformed from a humble fishing village into an important port city were rooted in vast pine and hemlock forests that fed a voracious lumber industry. Saw-wielding lumberjacks leveled ancient woodlands to build great cities like Chicago. Local sandstone quarries supplied fashionable brownstone. And its position as gateway to the Apostle Islands, now part of a designated national lakeshore, made it a favorite spot for the upper crust's magnificent summer homes.

But forests were mostly clear-cut before the turn of the century, leaving vast hillsides of mud and rubble devoid of almost any living vegetation. Timber barons closed down operations, abandoned opulent homes, and moved out west where there were more trees to harvest. By the 1920s the local economy hit rock bottom.

These days, however, the town is doing just fine as one of Wisconsin's favorite vacation playgrounds. In fact, there's so much to see and do, both in the village and around the islands, it might take a month's worth of weekends before you get your fill of this charming region. Here are some suggestions.

Summer

Take a walking tour to explore the town's striking 19th-century architecture. (Walking-tour maps with location keys are available at local stores.) You will see many grand homes that belonged to the rich and famous at the turn of the century; more than 50 buildings are listed on the National Register of Historic Places.

Among the most impressive is La Chateau Boutin, a massive 1907 Queen Anne Victorian at 7 Rice Avenue. Lumber baron Frank Boutin actually built this house as a surprise wedding gift for his new bride. But once she saw its location, on a hill overlooking the then clear-cut mud hills that stretched for miles around Bayfield, she refused to even step inside—and went back home to her parents in Minneapolis. Boutin soon followed.

Commercial fishing is still an important industry in Bayfield, though just a small remnant of a once-huge fleet. Come down to the docks before dawn and you'll see fishing boats heading out on the water, along with radiant sunrises. You can charter your own fishing boat or hire a captain for guided sightseeing sails. July and August are the calmest months on Lake Superior, perfect for lake-trout angling.

Or sail among the Apostle Islands on half-day to four-day captained cruises. Of course, you can learn to sail yourself at on-the-water classrooms offering sail-charter certification.

Back on shore, you'll learn that whitefish is a local delicacy, served at almost any restaurant in town. However, a more exotic treat is whitefish liver. Bayfield may be the only place on Lake Superior where commercial fishermen save the liver.

The Booth Cooperage Museum (at Washington and the lakefront) is the only working barrel factory in the state. Guided tours include demonstrations (most Saturdays and Sundays) of barrelmaking by coopers who heat, bend, and fit wooden staves much as their predecessors did a century ago. In this factory, five coopers once assembled nearly 75,000 high-quality barrels annually, each holding 115 pounds of salted fish.

Red Cliff Arts and Cultural Center, just north of Bayfield on State 13, preserves traditions for the Red Cliff band of Lake Superior Chippewas on their reservation here. Photo displays, artifacts, crafts, and paintings explore historic and contemporary Native American culture.

Better yet, visit during their annual July 4 powwow, a festival of dance, music, food, and art that draws Chippewa families from all over the Midwest. Newest festival wrinkle is an 18th-century living-history Indian village on Pointe De Tour (the tip of the peninsula).

For more down-to-earth pleasures, try your luck at the reservation's Isle Vista Casino, which includes plenty of blackjack tables, slot machines, big-money bingo, and live entertainment.

Bayfield has always been a haven for the arts. You can browse among scores of art galleries, boutiques, and specialty shops featuring everything from painters to weavers; or attend the Tri-State Arts & Crafts Fair at the end of July when artists set up displays in Memorial Park and along the town dock.

Another favorite is the Lake Superior Big Top Chautauqua, called "the Carnegie Hall of tent shows." Held at Mt. Ashwabay, three miles south of Bayfield, the June-through-September bash features 60 nights of concerts, plays, lectures, dramas, and historic musicals.

Apples are big business in the Bayfield area. Fifteen orchards thrive here, offering autumn U-pick adventures. Biggest celebration is the Apple Festival in early October, with parade, apple food booths, and live entertainment. Note that the region's mild, lake-effect climate provides a longer growing season than farms farther inland. As a result, you can enjoy midsummer U-pick crops of fresh strawberries, raspberries, blueberries, and cherries.

Apostle Islands National Lakeshore

Begin your island tour at the Headquarters Visitor Center in Bayfield, located inside the Old County Courthouse at Washington and Fourth Street. A short film introduces you to island history; park rangers can help you plan your island visit. You'll also learn about daily interpretive programs and guest lectures offered there and at other island locations.

It is just a 20-minute ferry boat ride from Bayfield to Madeline Island, the largest of the Apostle's 21 islands. It was named after the daughter of an Ojibwa chief and had a Native American population of nearly 12,000 as late as 1671. Then French explorers and missionaries arrived, beginning the island's era as headquarters for the fur trade. At the

Madeline Island Historical Museum, one block from the ferry dock, you'll see the site of the old American Fur Company trading post in La Pointe; it's housed in four log buildings under one roof. A 25-minute slide presentation illustrates the island's colorful history. Then wander among Chippewa handicrafts and artifacts of French traders, priests, and loggers.

Indian Burial Ground, half a mile from the docks, includes some grave markers nearly 200 years old. Most interesting are wooden "roofs" covering some grave sites. They were designed to shelter the dead and store food and clothing for the afterlife.

Perhaps the best swimming beach is at Big Bay State Park on the east shore, with a sandy beach and vistas of the rugged coastline. Just remember that Lake Superior is cold even in summer. A local once joked that he gauged water temperature by how long it takes a swimmer's feet to get numbed.

You can take three-hour to multiday cruises through the islands to learn more about their unique ecology. The Apostle Islands Cruise Service sails twice daily from Bayfield during July and August, and once daily in June and September. Cost is about $20 per person.

Make sure you visit Raspberry Island and its 1864 lighthouse station, now run by the National Park Service. One of the most breathtaking island lookouts is from the tower; at least five islands can be seen, including the 200-foot-high clay cliffs of Oak Island and the rolling hills of Minnesota's North Shore, some 35 miles away.

If you have an entire day or several days, be sure to take an inner-island shuttle boat to Sand Island. Hikers can trek the three-mile trail from the East Bay dock to the Sand Island lighthouse for guided tours of the lonely station. Or rent sea kayaks and take guided tours of the islands and the fabulous sea caves along the mainland shore. You can camp on five islands regularly serviced by excursion cruises or

Bayfield and the Apostle Islands

hop aboard water taxis to 13 more remote islands. However, almost half the camping expeditions take place on Stockton Island—which isn't surprising, considering its use as a seasonal campground for early inhabitants more than 3,000 years ago. National Park Service rangers lead guided walks here, exploring natural wonders, old fish camps, and quarry sites; evening campfire programs are also offered. Be aware that Stockton has a large black bear colony—about 23 animals.

Winter in the Apostles

Hardy souls seeking cold-weather adventures can find a paradise in the Bayfield region. Nearby Mount Ashwabay offers downhill skiing. Ice fishermen concoct their own tent cities out on the ice; ice stock-car races are popular on Sunday afternoons. Dogsledding is growing in popularity also, and Nordic skiers and snowmobilers can take advantage of miles of public trails winding through the inlands and islands.

For really wacky times, sample the February Frolics. Its two main events include ice golfing on Lake Superior and a five-mile run to Madeline Island and back to Bayfield across the iced-over waters.

FOR MORE INFORMATION

For Bayfield/Apostle Islands information, contact the Bayfield Chamber of Commerce, P.O. Box 138, Bayfield, WI 54814, 800-447-4094, and the Apostle Islands National Lakeshore Visitor Center, P.O. Box 721, Bayfield, WI 54814, 715-779-3397.

16

Native American Discoveries

DANCES WITH WOLVES, KEVIN COSTNER'S ACADEMY AWARD–
winning 1989 revisionist western about a post–Civil War
cavalry officer who abandons white society to become
"recivilized" by Sioux Indians, kick-started a growing
trend—the rediscovery by travelers of this country's Native
American heritage.

Today Native American historic sites, reservations, powwows, and special exhibits are enjoying an unflagging interest by people seeking to better understand these proud
cultures and enjoy their fascinating traditions. Midwest travelers have to search harder for Indian attractions (excluding
gambling casinos and bingo halls) than people in other parts
of the country. For example, Illinois has no federal or state
Indian reservations and few Indian-related special events.
Iowa's only reservation, the Sac and Fox Settlement, in
Tama, offers only a small powwow in August.

Wisconsin, however, is rich in Native American heritage.
At least six Indian nations live throughout the state: the
Menominee, Oneida, Potawatomi, Stockbridge-Munsee,
Winnebago, and Chippewa (Ojibwa). There are six bands
of Ojibwa, settled on reservations in Bad River, Lac Court
Oreilles, Lac du Flambeau, Mole Lake, St. Croix, and Red
Cliff.

Heritage highlights include everything from prehistoric Indian mounds and museum artifacts to powwows and dance ceremonials. Some spots might take no more than a few hours to enjoy; others merit an entire weekend.

Here are some of the most interesting Native American attractions in the state.

Tom-toms beat loudly and rhythmically. War whoops echo off rocky sandstone cliffs that form a natural rock amphitheater in the Upper Dells on the Wisconsin River. Then 40 Native Americans, dressed in traditional colorful costumes featuring feathered headdresses, intricate beadwork, bone necklaces, and jingling bells, glide out into the night performing the Hoop Dance, Eagle Dance, and Snake Dance. It's all part of the pageantry that surrounds the Stand Rock Indian Ceremonial, held nightly May through Labor Day in Wisconsin Dells.

Stand Rock is one of the few all-Indian shows in the country, comprised primarily of Winnebagos, whose ancestors used this location as a stopover during their semiannual migrations between summer and winter lodging grounds. The Winnebagos felt that the remarkable scenery of the Dells area contributed to their spiritual renewal during these journeys; soon they began performing traditional songs and dances as a religious rite.

That tradition continues today. Since 1929 dancers at Stand Rock have performed in a natural outdoor amphitheater among tall sandstone towers on the shore of the Wisconsin River. Performers range in age from five to 65, with children learning the steps at powwows and observing elders at practice. An added treat is five Zuni rainbow dancers from New Mexico who will add even more cultural diversity to the grand Winnebago performance.

Summer

Admission is charged; a combination ticket offers admission to both the ceremony and a round-trip Upper Dells nighttime boat ride. For information call 800-223-3557.

You can see Native American antiquities up close at the Winnebago Indian Museum, located at 3889 River Road, just outside the Dells. Besides some of the nation's finest contemporary Indian art and craftwork that's for sale, the museum chronicles Winnebago heritage, with archival photographs and rare artifacts that include traditional clothing, beadwork, and more. Call 608-254-2268.

The Land of the Menominee Powwow is usually held the last weekend in July or the first one in August on the Menominee Indian Reservation in Keshena, Wisconsin. Native American writers have called it "one of the main [Native American] cultural events of the year in the Midwest."

More than 1,000 dancers from as far away as Oklahoma, Montana, and Canada will gather in Woodland Bowl, a natural amphitheater surrounded by towering white pines, to compete in fancy dancing, grass dancing, and traditional dancing competitions. Visitors can also sample Native American foods like fry bread, wild rice, and venison burgers. If you want even more, tour the tribe's historic logging museum, visit the Vegas-style casino and bingo hall, or take a lazy raft float on the Wolf River. Daily and weekend passes are available. Call 715-799-5100.

The Oneida Nation Museum, seven miles west of Green Bay in Oneida, boasts one of the largest ongoing exhibitions of Oneida history and artifacts in the world. Displays include ceremonial dress, dioramas, and cultural exhibits that explain tribal lifestyles, including important roles for women—they got to choose the new chief, a kind of suffrage unheard of in "civilized" European societies even when Columbus invaded the New World. Especially note-

Native American Discoveries

worthy is the hand-on activities room where kids can feel furs and beadwork, heft a war club, and beat on ceremonial drums.

Outside, you can tour a reconstructed, full-size Oneida stockade village, see costumed interpreters pound corn into meal, watch tomahawk-throwing demonstrations, listen to bird and animal calls, and discover secrets of Native American medicine at the herb garden.

Then step inside a 42-foot longhouse to feel hides stretched by the sun, grind corn yourself, and listen to an Indian storyteller. Admission is charged. Call 414-869-2768.

You may have to do a little hiking, but it's worth the walk to Gullickson's Glen near Black River Falls. It boasts prehistoric Indian petroglyphs etched on the sandstone walls of a deep ravine. Figures include a thunderbird, buffalo, eagle dancer, and more. The site is administered by the Wisconsin Historical Society, in Madison. Call 608-264-6400.

More than 5,000 prehistoric Indian mounds are located in Wisconsin. In the city of Sheboygan, you can take a self-guided "mound trail" that passes 18 earthen effigy mounds at the Sheboygan Indian Mound Park (Twelfth Street and Panther Avenue); the mounds are listed on the National Register of Historic Places. Call 414-459-3444.

Guidebooks also can help locate Native American touring spots. Among the best are:

- *Discover Indian Reservations*, edited by Veronica E. Tiller (Council Publications, $19.95), which describes activities, including gambling, that take place on 35 Midwest reservations, mostly in Minnesota, Michigan, and Wisconsin.

- *The Traveler's Guide to Native America—The Great Lakes Region*, by Hayward Allen (North Woods Press, Inc., $16.95), which offers extensive historical information and a rundown of Indian attractions in Wisconsin, Illinois, Indiana, Michigan, Minnesota, and Ohio.

- *Indian America*, by Eagle/Walking Turtle (John Muir Publications, $17.95), including history from the Native American viewpoint, striking archival photographs, and directions on where to find ceremonies, arts, crafts, museums, powwows, and historic sites.

Native American Discoveries

17

Circus World Museum

BARABOO

"LADIES AND GENTLEMAN!" THE RINGMASTER SHOUTED. "YOU are about to see an astronomical amalgam of astounding antics that will absolutely amaze you. Get ready for thrills and excitement like you've never seen before.

"Presenting our own Big Top Circus."

That's just the beginning of the colorful pageantry at Circus World Museum in Baraboo, home to summerlong live circus shows as well as the largest collection of antique, hand-carved circus wagons and other big-top artifacts and memorabilia in the world. It is also a national historic landmark.

But why is the circus in Baraboo? More than a century ago, the hometown Ringling brothers launched an overland wagon circus show. By 1884 the brothers decided to return to Baraboo each winter, both to rebuild their circus equipment and expand their acts at these off-season headquarters.

Around the turn of the century, it was not surprising to see elephants marching down the streets of Baraboo. All kinds of exotic animals were housed in brick buildings lining Water Street. Other buildings were used in which to train tigers, camels, elephants, and horses for new circus acts.

In 1906 the Ringlings purchased the renowned Barnum & Bailey Circus. Now they managed the two largest circuses in the world, each with hundreds of animal menageries, sideshows, performers, and each circus offering a grand, free street parade. After the 1918 season, the Ringlings decided to combine the two circuses, and they moved to new winter headquarters in Bridgeport, Connecticut. Eventually, they moved again, settling in Venice, Florida, their home base today.

Baraboo's big-top legacy is celebrated at the Circus World Museum, spread out over 50 fun-filled acres along the banks of the Baraboo River and crammed with the colorful artifacts of Baraboo's circus history.

Throughout the year, visitors to the modern Irvin Feld Exhibit Hall are tickled by circus lore and legend. You'll marvel at the world's largest collection of antique circus parade wagons, with more than 150 of these intricately hand-carved, glittering works of art displayed in all their glory. See the Ringling Bell Wagon, with its massive cathedral chime bells; the Bostock Band Chariot, oldest surviving circus wagon in the world; the huge Barnum & Bailey's Two Hemispheres, the largest circus parade wagon ever built; and two restored masterpieces—the Pawnee Bill Bandwagon, which boasts elaborate carvings of Columbus discovering America, and the elegant Swan Bandwagon built in Baraboo more than a century ago.

The museum also holds the world's largest circus-history archive, with unparalleled collections of circus lithographs, photos, and other treasures of American circus lore.

During the "live show" season (from May through mid-

September), the "Greatest Show on Earth" is reborn with all the pageantry and excitement of the circus of yesteryear, with big-top performances daily in mid-July through mid-August. Spotlighted are world-class performers, including heartstopping, acrobatic high-wire artistry: performers dance, skip, jump-rope, and leapfrog over each other while dangling 30 feet in the air—without a net! They present more: death-defying forward dives on the flying trapeze; African elephant acrobats; astounding bareback riding feats; incredible balancing, tossing, and twirling acts; musical mayhem clown acts. Fearless lion tamers risk life and limb while tending to ferocious felines.

There's also a 20-minute giant-screen presentation of superstar circus animal trainer Gunther Gebel-Williams, who was with Barnum & Bailey for more than 20 years, offered throughout the day. And the "Mysteries of Magic" show will mesmerize you with incredible illusions.

Of course, you can become part of the circus, too. Climb aboard an elephant for a ride around an outdoor big-top ring. Enjoy a spin on the antique carousel, or hop on a trolley for a tour of Baraboo's historic circus sites.

Little kids (and adults, too) like to walk through holding tents where lions, giraffe, and other exotic animals are kept when not performing. More fun activities include circus train-loading demonstrations, clown shows, street parades, and street calliope concerts.

Two special summer-season events deserve mention. Wagon Roll-Out Days offers a chance to take photographs of some of the museum's unrivaled circus wagons with Circus World performers in full costume. And during the Great Circus Train Loading, you'll see Percheron draft horses load 75 antique circus wagons onto the Great Circus Train as it prepares for its two-day journey for the mid-July Great Circus Parade, which rolls through downtown Mil-

Circus World Museum

waukee—another spectacular circus event that shouldn't be missed.

But just remember, every day is circus day at Circus World Museum.

For More Information

For admission prices and information, contact Circus World Museum, 426 Water Street, Baraboo, WI 53913, 608-356-8341. For 24-hour Circus World information, call its Info-Line, 608-356-0800.

Summer

18

Cheese League NFL Training Camps

SOUTHWESTERN WISCONSIN

DIE-HARD FOOTBALL FANS CALL IT HEAVEN. PLAYERS CALL IT hell. Others simply call it the "Cheese League."

It's the annual ritual of National Football League summer training camps. Wisconsin has four Cheese League towns that host NFL teams while they hold scrimmages and play exhibition games from July through mid-August to prepare for the championship season and a chance to win the Super Bowl. Fans from all over the Midwest flock to the practice field of their favorite team, watching their heroes get into playing shape.

Visitors can view open practices and scrimmages, which generally run from 9:00 A.M. to 3:00 P.M. during irregular intervals daily; some teams have even begun night sessions to avoid searing summer heat.

For the last decade, the biggest draw has been the Chicago Bears, whose team of cocky characters actually concocted the most lopsided Super Bowl victory (January 1986) in the history of the game. Led by volatile coach Mike Ditka, who used to conduct training sessions while riding a customized "Ditka-mobile" (golf cart), the Bears generated all kinds of attention.

While they still train at the University of Wisconsin at Platteville, located in the extreme southwestern portion of the state, things have pretty much calmed down. Most players from that 1985 championship team have retired; their replacements haven't shown the drive, ability, or swagger of their predecessors; and even Ditka is gone, fired after the 1992 season.

Current coach Dick Jauron's camp has more of a calm, professional atmosphere, compared with Dikta's "kick-your-mother-in-the-shins" sneer-and-snarl style. Yet Chicago fans, a four-hour-drive away from their heroes, still come here by the droves; perhaps it'll take more than several poor seasons to completely wash away the aura of that Super Bowl win, now nearly a decade old.

What's the attraction, besides watching "grown" men sweat, grunt, and hit each other in the blazing sun? Lots of times, it's just a matter of reaching across the practice-field ropes to grab an autograph or ask for a photo with your favorite player. You can't do that at Chicago's Soldier Field, where the Bears play their regular season games.

Platteville's business community joins in the Bear-mania. Stores continue the practice of "adopting" a Bears player, then decorating windows with pictures of the chosen warrior. Local watering holes, most located on Second Street near Main, are sometimes frequented by players, giving fans another chance to mingle with their heroes. (Orville T.'s and The Hoist House are rumored to be favorite Bears' hangouts.) For restaurants, try Timbers, the Roundtree, and Pizzeria Uno (for Chicago-style pizza).

Nearby, two other NFL teams go through the rigors of summer camp: the New Orleans Saints, at the University of Wisconsin at La Crosse; and the Kansas City Chiefs, at the University of Wisconsin at River Falls.

However, the home-state Green Bay Packers are the other big Cheese League draw. Venerable Lambeau Field and its practice greens are the site for the "green and gold" to bang heads during summer sessions. An added attraction is the Green Bay Packer Hall of Fame, located directly across the street from Lambeau Field. It is a "must-see" for any football fan, especially if they want to relive the days when the Vince Lombardi–led Pack dominated the NFL. Besides exhibits showcasing team history, coaches, and players, you can suit up in Packer style and kick a field goal or throw a pass. You'll also love the "football bloopers" film, and you can test your football acumen during computer football quizzes.

FOR MORE INFORMATION

For more information about the Chicago Bears' summer training camp, contact the Platteville Chamber of Commerce, 97 East Main Street, Platteville, WI 53818, 608-348-8888; Green Bay Packers, 800-236-3976; Kansas City Chiefs, 715-425-2533; and the New Orleans Saints, 800-658-9424. Or contact the Wisconsin Division of Tourism, P.O. Box 7606, Madison, WI 53707, 800-432-8747.

Cheese League NFL Training Camps

.

19

Experimental Aircraft Association Fly-In

OSHKOSH

A SQUADRON OF B-17 BOMBERS ROARS OVERHEAD, FLYING IN combat formation. The noise is deafening and terrifying. It is the largest single Midwest flyby of rare warbirds that helped defeat Hitler's army since World War II.

A sleek navy F-14 cruises by next, wiggling its wings to the crowd. This is the *Top Gun* jet, a pulsating war machine that has no equal in a dogfight.

Hovering just above the airfield as if weightless is the Harrier, a marine jet possessing mammoth brute force. That this high-tech monster can both take off and land in a gentle vertical movement is beyond belief.

Getting ready for takeoff at the end of the runway is the B-29, largest bomber ever built by any nation. The B-29 dropped atomic bombs on Hiroshima and Nagasaki; this is the last one in flying condition.

Every summer during the last week in July and spilling into August, the Experimental Aircraft Association's (EAA) International Fly-In and Sport Aviation Exhibition lures more than 15,000 planes of all types to this city's tiny Wittman Field for the biggest air show in the country, not to mention the death-defying aerobatic stunts from international flight crews, wing walkers, and daredevils; antique biplanes and crazy home-built contraptions; historic classic planes; and the crowd favorite—warbirds.

One year the Fly-In drew more planes in one spot than ever before in history, according to EAA officials. Another time, about 7 percent of the entire U.S. aircraft fleet was present at the show, not to mention the million people who set up lawn chairs and beach blankets along the flight line to watch dizzying loop-de-loops, dazzling precision maneuvers, and mock military dogfights.

Opening day usually draws upward of a quarter-million people alone. Special guests have included everyone from top military brass to the original seven *Mercury* astronauts who flew nonstop around the world in their *Voyageur* aircraft.

Daily air shows promise to be heart-pounding thrillers. You're likely to see B-1 and B-52 bombers, air force F-18 jet fighters, P-40 Flying Tigers with their famous shark teeth nose, Japanese Zeros, and more. International flying aces often include the U.S. Air Force Thunderbirds and the Red Hawks of the Italian Air Force. There'll be biplane barnstormers performing nail-biting stunts, and all kinds of classic, antique, homebuilts, and ultra-lights—weird, winsome, and wacky.

People watching is another favorite Fly-In pastime, and the Fly Market is a good place to do it. More than 600 exhibitors offer all kinds of goodies, from powerful new Porsche aircraft engines and dirigible kits to goofy hats sporting wind socks and propellers or T-shirts proclaiming every patriotic jingoism ever coined. NASA often has a major high-tech aerospace display. You can purchase your own Lear jet here, too.

Hundreds of seminars, forums, and workshops are open to the public and EAA members alike. They've featured top NASA scientists, Federal Aviation Administration officials, aeronautics researchers and designers, and "regular guys" talking on a wide range of topics. You even can learn how to build your own fiberglass plane in a hands-on construction session.

It's a half-mile walk or a free shuttle-bus ride from the airfield to the EAA Air Museum, where you'll see hundreds of dramatic displays of historic aircraft in one of the country's finest collections. The Air Adventure Theater's Vista-vision screen with sense-around stereo sound shakes and rumbles moviegoers watching wild aerobatics as if they were in the cockpit themselves.

FOR MORE INFORMATION

Daily air shows usually begin by early afternoon, lasting about three hours. Though warbirds can be seen in static (on-the-ground) displays, mock dogfights and military manuevers take place during only one or two special shows; call ahead for details. Try to make it on weekdays; weekend shows often draw upward of 300,000 people. Arrive early or risk getting caught in a massive traffic jam and missing the beginning of the air show. Unless you're a diehard, don't attend only on the final day; lots of planes and exhibitors leave early. There are daily admission fees and show-length passes, with student and senior rates available. Small children, accompanied by parents, are admitted free. For a schedule of events and information, contact Experimental Aircraft Association Museum, 3000 Poberezny Drive, Oshkosh, WI 54901, 920-426-4800.

Experimental Aircraft Association Fly-In

20

Old World Wisconsin

EAGLE

A PIONEER WOMAN HUNCHES OVER A BIG BLACK KETTLE BUB-
bling with boiling hot water and lye soap. With a long stick
she swirls a calico dress through the potion, then hangs it
high on a tree branch to drip dry.

"Laundry day is real special," she says. "Usually we just
brush the dirt off our clothes. But every couple of months
we have to boil them clean."

This settler "lives" on the Fossebrekke Farm, one of the
oldest buildings at Old World Wisconsin, a 576-acre living-
history museum in Eagle. As one of the museum's historic
site interpreters, she wears period clothes and tackles typical daily tasks of pioneer homesteaders.

The farm's authentic Norwegian cabin dates to 1841,
when it served as home to namesake Knute, his wife, and
their three children. Its 400 square feet of living space are
dank and dreary.

"Last winter we had 17 people living with us," she says.
"Wasn't too bad. And when summer came, we got to take
our yearly bath down in the river."

Old World Wisconsin is a step back in time to Wisconsin's
pioneer immigrant heritage. "Settlers" (costumed interpreters) inhabit 11 ethnic farms and an 1870s crossroads vil-

lage, performing regular chores and providing a glimpse of what life was like on 19th-century homesteads.

Visitors wander through 50 historic buildings actually built by Wisconsin pioneers and rescued by modern-day historians from all over the state—the shores of Lake Superior in the north to farm fields near Milwaukee in the south. Each building has been carefully researched and restored to match the setting of its original locale.

At the 1896 Raspberry School, found in Bayfield County, a teacher runs students (that's you, parents and kids alike, who sit in school desks) through exercises of readin', writin', and arithmetic in the one-room schoolhouse.

"Teaching isn't easy," she explains. "Besides minding children that might not want to be here, teachers can't be married or engaged, wear bright-colored clothes, or ride in a buggy with a man other than their father or brother, and must be inside by 8:00 P.M. every night. And I'm paid only ten dollars a month, plus free room and board."

Walk a winding path to the 1894 Ketola Farm, and you'll learn that a sauna was an essential building on a Finnish homestead. "People would climb in here at least twice a week," says the site interpreter. "Temperatures could get as high as 200 degrees, but you'd have to open window vents or else you'd smell like smoked bacon."

In the farmhouse, another settler is making crust for apple pie. This dairy farm, built in three stages from 1894 to 1900 in Oulu (near Bayfield), was lived in (as is—no electricity, gas, telephone) by three bachelor brothers until 1968.

Come to Old World Wisconsin during the Midsummer Festival in mid-June to enjoy a special treat: the spectacle of a centuries-old Scandinavian hoedown celebrating the longest day of the year. Held at the Danish, Finnish, and Norwegian homesteads, the bash features traditional entertainment performed by costumed artists.

A colorful Maypole celebration on the visitors center

Summer

green is a highlight. The Maypole (from the Swedish *maja*, meaning decorated with greens and flowers) is a tall spruce tree stripped of branches and adorned with flowers and flags. Costumed Swedish, Norwegian, and Finnish dancers entertain along with a Scandinavian chorus.

Then visit historic 19th-century buildings, decorated with wildflowers and birch branches, with Scandinavian settlers preparing traditional ethnic dishes for their own Maypole holiday picnic.

Be sure to explore the museum's other ethnic homesteads, including the Kruza House, a Polish farm home built in 1884 displaying unique stovewood architecture. It held both family and prized chickens.

At the Crossroads Village, which portrays an 1870s Wisconsin settlement catering to "town" residents, step inside the Sanford House, an elegant Greek Revival home, typical of what a prosperous Yankee farmer would have lived in by 1860.

Pass by the 1886 Grotelueschen Blacksmith Shop, and you'll see a burly smithy ply his trade. The 1839 St. Peter's Church, the first Catholic church in Milwaukee, has a consecrated altar, so Catholic weddings still take place here throughout the year.

You can get food and refreshments at the Clausing Barn, an 1897 octagonal structure containing a cafeteria-style restaurant. The visitors center, housed in the 1841 Ramsey Barn, offers 19th-century reproductions for purchase and a video theater.

Other Old World Wisconsin annual festivals include Sheep Shearing, in mid-May, when sheep are shorn and wool is cleaned, dyed, and fashioned into fabric; Centennial Independence Day, on July 4, an 1876 small-town celebration of Uncle Sam's birthday complete with costume parade, music, ethnic foods, greased-pole climb, and kid games; Harvest Days, in early August, when farmers harvest grain with

Old World Wisconsin

horse-drawn threshers and attend a temperance rally in the village; and the Heirloom Garden Fair, at the end of August, an oldtime country fair with fruits and vegetables on display, all grown from 19th-century seed varieties.

While historic buildings are closed in the winter, the grounds open during snow season for cross-country skiing. So you'll literally ski through Wisconsin history.

FOR MORE INFORMATION

Admission is charged; family rates are available. There is no extra charge for Midsummer Festival or other special activities. Trams (extra charge) offer rides to museum homesteads. The museum is open June through October, daily; call for winter ski dates and times. Old World Wisconsin is located on State 67, about 20 miles southwest of Milwaukee. Contact the museum at 5103 W37890 Highway 67, Eagle, WI 53119, 414-594-6300.

21

Lake Geneva

THE EIGHT-MILE-LONG BODY OF WATER THAT CHIEF BIG FOOT and his Potawatomi Indians called *Kish-Way-Kee-Tow* (clear water) has beckoned big-city weekenders, many from Chicago, for more than a century. Today, 5,300-acre Lake Geneva remains a tranquil antidote to the pressures of life in the fast lane.

Maybe the best way to get a spring or summer feel for Lake Geneva is by riding the waves. Head to the Geneva Cruise Line's Riviera Docks, located on Wrigley Drive, where the boat company offers all kinds of special May-through-October floats and cruises.

My daughters, Kate and Dayne, love the ice-cream social float, a 75-minute cruise that includes a narrated tour of the lake and a sundae made with Wisconsin ice cream.

Another favorite is the Mark Twain Dinner Cruise, with a Mark Twain impersonator aboard the *Belle of the Lake*, an 1890s lake-steamer replica, sharing the writer's unique insights on riverboat life, human nature, small towns, and bad habits. These special afternoon and night cruises are usually scheduled June to September.

Perhaps the best choice during blazing fall colors is the cruise line's combination "hike and float" champagne brunch tour. Start out early in the morning after buying your boat ticket at the downtown docks and trek a footpath that encircles the lake. It's actually a remnant of an old Indian trail that once connected several Potawatomi camps ringing the water.

The scenery along the way is not only autumn pretty, but also reveals vistas of grand mansions and spectacular "summer cottages" built primarily by movers and shakers of early Chicago mercantile history—including the likes of Montgomery Ward (of department-store fame) and William Wrigley (chewing gum, Wrigley Field, and the former owner of those lovable losers, the Chicago Cubs).

It takes about four hours to leisurely walk eight miles to Williams Bay. You have to get there before noon for pick-up by the Geneva Cruise Line boat. Then you'll enjoy a refreshing champagne toast and brunch as you float back to the Lake Geneva docks. (If you don't want to hop aboard a boat, just continue along the path. It stretches for 26 miles around Lake Geneva.)

You shouldn't pass up a town tradition—a float on the Lake Geneva mail boat, one of the few remaining marine mail-deliveries left in the United States. What makes it especially interesting is that the boat never actually stops: a mail girl must jump onto the dock, deposit mail into boxes posted at the pier, and leap back aboard. So far I've never seen one of these dashing lasses drop into the drink.

Mail boats run June 15 through September 15, seven days a week, rain or shine. (The mail must go through!) Reservations are required, so be sure to call ahead. Geneva Lake Cruise Line's special family rates offer 10 to 15 percent discounts on fares. Call 800-558-5911.

For exercise and education at the same time, sign up for one of the summer's shore-path walks sponsored by the Geneva Lake Conservancy. These free guided tours include wildflower, prairie plant, and fen tours. For a schedule call 414-248-3358.

More down-to-earth fun can be enjoyed at Geneva Lakes Riding Stable, just west of State 67 and 50. One-ton draft horses pull hay wagons along trails of rolling hills and hardwood forests; families with older kids can saddle up for trail rides. Call 414-728-6560.

Shopping is another Lake Geneva mainstay, with more than 20 specialty shops and boutiques dotting downtown storefronts. Two of my Main Street favorites are K. J. Flemings Ltd., where daughters Kate and Dayne search through Irish handicrafts for a gift suitable for their County Armagh Irish grandma; and Overland Sheepskin, where they can try on sheepskin coats and cowboy hats.

And after a hard day's shopping (you can use any other excuse), it is almost impossible to resist the delectable treats at Annie's Ice Cream Parlor, another Main Street staple.

If you'd rather leave the driving and walking to others, you can explore Lake Geneva aboard The Trolley, a red-and-green turn-of-the-century "bus" that offers narrated tours gushing with insights about the town's history, shopping, and restaurants—all gleaned from the seat of your pants. It operates seven days per week, May through September; admission is charged.

Two other nearby attractions can add fun to your Lake Geneva visit. Only on Saturdays you can tour the University of Chicago's Yerkes Observatory on State 67 in Williams Bay. Free hour-long tours offer a peek at the world's largest refracting telescope. Call 414-245-5555.

Families should head out to Green Meadows Children's Farm in Waterford. Two-hour guided tours include peeks at more than 200 farm animals, pony rides, tractor-drawn hayrides, a cow-milking session, and a chance to get some hands-on cuddling with everything from pigs, cows, and goats to sheep, chickens, and donkeys. An admission fee is charged. Call 414-534-2891.

For More Information

For more Lake Geneva information (along with mailing addresses for the above attractions), contact Lake Geneva Convention and Visitors Bureau, 201 Wrigley Drive, Lake Geneva, WI 53147, 414-248-4416 or 800-345-1020.

Summer

22

Wisconsin State Fair

WEST ALLIS

YOU DON'T HAVE TO KNOW GARTH BROOKS FROM GOMER Pyle to have fun at the Wisconsin State Fair. And while it won't hurt to bone up on a few episodes of "Andy Griffith" (to say nothing of "Green Acres") before downing a dishful of state-fair corn pone, there's enough slick shtick to make fairgoers from the big city feel at home.

In fact, Wisconsin's 11-day agri-bash, which opens the first Thursday in August annually, may boast the most cosmopolitan ambience of any state fair in the country. That's because the fairgrounds are located in West Allis, a suburb of Milwaukee (the state's largest city). And it draws more than 100,000 folks from Chicago, located only 90 miles south of here.

Though yearly attendance hovers near one million people, officials always hope to lure even more visitors to State Fair Park during the farm fest with the promise of free entertainment at 19 stages, big-name country and western and pop music entertainers on the grandstand's main stage, 500 commercial exhibits housed in air-conditioned buildings (hawking everything from vibrating rocking chairs to belt buckles as large as the state of Rhode Island), daily parades and nightly fireworks, and up-close peeks at some of the Midwest's best blue-ribbon dairy and beef cattle, draft horses, sheep, goats, swine, rabbits, and poultry. (However, excitement does not include a reenactment of the attraction that catapulted the 1902 state fair into the realm of legend—when two railroad locomotives chugged at each other head-on until they collided in a screeching heap of mangled metal.)

These are among the highlights of the state fair. Wisconsin political notables often perform "soda jerk" duties during the fair by selling more than 11 flavors of Wisconsin moo juice (milk) at the "Superb Milkhouse." Be sure to witness at least one livestock judging contest; more than 25,000 ribbons will be awarded to barnyard hotshots during the fair.

The International Bazaar is another crowd-pleaser, boasting 95 vendors with authentic imported merchandise from places as far away as Thailand. Oriental Marketplace is a showplace for the wares, entertainment, and cuisine of six Oriental cultures.

The Comedy Cabaret features local comics, magicians, and illusionists daily at the Activity Dome. Also count on daily pig races (a perennial favorite with fairgoers), 4-H singers, high-school bands, a ride- and game-filled midway carnival, kids' petting zoo, cooking demonstrations, spelling bees, arts and crafts displays, and more.

Music lovers won't be disappointed by the fair's free lineup of old rockers and smooth crooners. Past performers have included everyone from the Platters and Ink Spots to Herman's Hermits and Mitch Ryder & the Detroit Wheels. The hottest big-name performers appear on the grandstand's main stage; tickets for these shows are extra. Count on seeing the likes of Willie Nelson, Garth Brooks, Billy Ray Cyrus, Alabama, Kenny Rogers, Foreigner, and the Beach Boys.

However, several observers believe all this state fair hype is just an excuse to sell what might be the world's most delicious cream puffs. Since the 1920s, the Wisconsin Bakers

Association has conjured up its secret recipe to make and sell more than 200,000 of these Dairy State delicacies each year. The light and wispy puff pastries, filled with mounds of fresh whipped cream, are easily the fair's favorite pig-out treat; last year, about 25 cream puffs were sold every minute of the fair. So you might want to head to the East Wing of the park's Exhibit Hall whenever that sweet tooth starts to ache.

FOR MORE INFORMATION

Admission is charged; there's also a fee for parking. Gates open daily at 8:00 A.M., buildings at 9:00 A.M., the midway at 10:00 A.M.; the park closes at 11:00 P.M. Wisconsin State Fair Park is located at 84th Street and Greenfield Avenue in West Allis. For more information contact Wisconsin State Fair Park, Milwaukee/West Allis, WI 53214, 414-266-7000.

Wisconsin State Fair

23

Wacky Festival Weekends

FORGET PARIS, STRUGGLING ARTISTS, AND SIDEWALK CAFÉS. Scratch Florida's Disney World with Mickey, Minnie, and the gang.

Instead, think Twin-O-Rama in Cassville, Loon Day in Mercer, Ridiculous Daes in Rhinelander, The Hot Pepper Festival in North Hudson, and the state Cow Chip Throwing Championship in Prairie du Sac.

Odd little festivals throughout Wisconsin promise quirky pleasure for weekenders willing to explore winding back roads to such small-town amusements. So load up the family wagon and get ready for some major laughs. (But before driving to attend an event, be sure to call ahead and verify festival dates.)

You'll see double at Twin-O-Rama, Cassville's mid-July weekend-long paean to multiple births. Nearly 450 twins and triplets gather from across the country to celebrate their better halves. "There's always lots of ogling going on," say fest organizers.

I'll bet. Contests honor the youngest and oldest twins, those who live farthest apart, toddlers, and other categories. "You'll look at some and figure they're not twins, looking so opposite," observes a longtime Cassville resident who always attends the twin fest. "But maybe it's something in the water." For more information, contact Cassville Civic Club, Box 576, Cassville, WI 53806, 608-725-5180; Twin-O-Rama, 608-725-5110.

Ridiculous Daes in Rhinelander, another mid-July weekend bash, can get "very ridiculous," according to town officials. Downtown streets are closed off, shops offer bargains at ridiculous prices, and people dress in ridiculous costumes. One year's fashion-plate winner came dressed as a toilet. You've got to admit that's pretty ridiculous. Contact the Chamber of Commerce, 135 South Stevens Street, P.O. Box 795-W, Rhinelander, WI 54501, 715-362-7464.

Early August usually heralds the coming of Loon Day in Mercer, which already honors the bird with a 16-foot-tall statue outside its chamber of commerce building. During the celebration's loon-calling contest, town residents "stand on the stage and do things with their hands and mouth" trying to imitate the bird's eerie wail. Contact the Chamber of Commerce, Box 368, Mercer, WI 54547, 715-476-2389.

North Hudson serves up a Hot Pepper Festival the first weekend in August, with a pepper-eating contest as a featured attraction. Five-person teams gulp down an entire pound of fiery peppers: the record is 13 seconds. Some contestants prepare by drinking something that allows the pepper to slide right down, according to a former contest official. Others use liquids to coat their tongues so that the peppers won't burn their mouths.

However, a large contingent of pepper eaters contends that "lots of beer helps." But don't hot peppers on top of cold beer cause problems? It seems a few people have gotten sick onstage, officials admit. They are simply disqualified. Contact the Chamber of Commerce and Tourism Bureau, 512 Third Street, P.O. Box 438, Hudson, WI 54016, 715-386-8411 or 800-657-6775.

If you have ever been accused of slinging the bull, you might be a natural for the Wisconsin State Cow Chip

Throwing Championship in Prairie du Sac, usually held the first weekend in September. You'll get two tosses using dried cow chips (what'd you expect?), each at least six inches in diameter. The state record is 225 feet for men, 133 feet for women. Winners advance to the national cow-chip throwing finals. Contact the Sauk-Prairie Chamber of Commerce, P.O. Box 7, Sauk City, WI 53583, 608-643-4168.

There are plenty of other wacky Wisconsin festivals that you might want to check out throughout the year:

The Polar Bear Swim, January 1, in Sheboygan, welcomes anybody willing to brave Lake Michigan's frigid waters and take a New Year's dip. More than 300 swimmers, apparently with ice water in their veins, often participate. Call 920-457-9495.

A Turkey Seminar, early February in Sauk City, is for fowl fans who wish to compete with world-champion callers in a turkey-calling contest or who just want to find out more about America's Thanksgiving treat. Call 608-643-2433.

Golf on Ice, mid-March in Iron River, will guarantee duffers they won't find themselves burdened with a single sand trap—but those snowdrifts can be murder. Call 715-372-8879.

Ice Bowling, mid-March in Sheboygan, is a huge bowling tournament held on solid ice; at least you won't throw any gutter balls. Call 414-452-6443.

The Milk Jug Regatta, mid-June in Minocqua, features races among boats made from plastic milk jugs. Call 800-446-6784.

A Mini Grand Prix Auto Race, mid-June in Oshkosh, offers some Indy-style excitement, with mini grand-prix cars zooming around a Continental-inspired race track reaching speeds of nearly 30 mph. Call 920-235-1980.

The World Champion Snowmobile Water Cross and Summerfest, mid-July in Grantsburg, a different kind of sport,

Wacky Festival Weekends

features five classes of snowmobiles racing on open water. Call 715-463-2331.

Journey into the Wild Swine Time Pig Races, an end-of-July weekend in Hazelhurst, with porker sprints and other hog-wild fun. Or try the Annual Weed Sale, mid-September in Brookfield, where you can purchase every kind of pesky weed that's ever infested your garden. Seriously, weeds and wildflowers are used to create baskets, door hangings, and other crafty items. Call 414-781-9560.

For More Information

Wisconsin's several celebrations take place all year long, contact the Wisconsin Division of Tourism at P.O. Box 7606, Madison, WI 53707-7606, 800-432-8747 or 800-372-2737.

Summer

24

Cool Car Classics

ELKHART LAKE AND MADISON

WANT TO WANDER WISCONSIN BACK ROADS WITH YOUR TOP
down, cruising some of this dairy-studded state's most
scenic highways? Or would you rather take a race-car
"speedway" tour?

Then put the pedal to the metal and get to these cool car
classics.

Sports Car Cruising

Ever sit in your recliner watching the X-Games on ESPN2 and
say to yourself, "Boy, I wish I could do something crazy like
that for a change." Here's your chance, a once-in-a-lifetime
thrill that takes you to some of the most famous race-car
tracks in mid-America, where you can drive your own car
over the same pavement that has been marked with the
peeled rubber of stars like A. J. Foyt and Big Daddy Garlitz.

Just sign up for the annual Wisconsin Sports Car & GT
Classic Tour, usually held in mid-June and billed as "the
world's premier Euro-style road tour." One of the most exciting classic four-wheel whirls ever started out in Union

Grove, Wisconsin, at Great Lakes Dragaway, moved to the Slinger International Speedway in Slinger and crossed the finish line at Road America in Elkhart Lake.

"Let's face it—driving your own sporty car on three of the world's greatest racing circuits is as close to the X-Games as most of us ever care to get," said Gary Knowles, cofounder with Alex McDonell of a number of popular summer and fall auto tours that wind through the scenic backroads of the Dairy State, visit some of the world's greatest race tracks, and offer opportunities for these owners to display to the public the "rolling car museum" collection.

This Euro-style road tour is a four-day, noncompetitive run open to anybody owning any kind of vintage sports car, sport-edition vehicle, or grand-touring car. In the past, everything from the smallest English Austin Mini to sleek Corvettes and Porsches have been part of the automotive lineup. One sports-car enthusiast even shipped his vehicle over from Japan to make the run.

"The WSCC is for all people who love cars and recreational driving," Knowles explained. "They've spent lots of time at race tracks pressing their noses to the fence. And they want some adventure but at very low risk.

"And they know that the best way to appreciate a good car is to get behind the wheel and drive it. The WSCC maximizes opportunities for these recreational driving enthusiasts to do just that."

Tour locations and destinations can vary from year to year. One began in Union Grove, home to Great Lakes Dragaway, famed for fast cars and one of the loudest and most annoying radio commercials in history. But there's no doubt that this racing den provided one of the biggest thrills on the WSCC.

In fact, participants actually were allowed to go on the track, position their cars off the timing line, watch the lights signal "go" on the starting tower, and be tested for a "driver

Summer

reaction"—to see how quickly they'd react to start a race down the dragstrip.

The next thrill took place at the Slinger International Speedway in Slinger, which is home to the world's fastest quarter-mile track. Maybe that's because the track is banked an astounding 33 degrees. WSCC cars were allowed to do a lap on this incredible track, a lap which not only excites drivers but also commemorates the world's first auto race, held in Wisconsin in 1878.

Cars and drivers always finish at Road America in Elkhart Lake, site of some of the world's greatest Indy-style racing. Not only does the WSCC receive admission to the annual June Sprints (one of the top races in the country), but it enjoys 30 minutes of track touring time on the famed layout.

How exciting is all this drive time? "They (drivers) get out of their cars with their eyes bulging, their hands shaking, and their hearts pounding like jackhammers," McDonell said. "You can almost put your hand on the fender and take their pulse!"

Besides driving time on some of the world's greatest tracks, other WSCC highlights include a Euro-backroads run, this one called the Kettle Moraine Grand Prix. A road run (1999's was called "Beat the Devil through the Holy Land" because it traveled through a section of eastern Wisconsin known for its tiny hamlets sporting Biblical names), and Paddock Passes to those Road America June Sprints.

Cost for the four-day tour is about $115 per car, which includes the driver and one passenger; additional passengers are $25. A special two-day Executive Privilege Package joins the tour midway through the festivities and continues through Road America; call to learn the cost of this option.

Note that lodging and meals are not included with the participation fee; the WSCC has reserved blocks of rooms at selected hotels, available at the hotels on a first-come, first-served basis to tour members.

Cool Car Classics

One other thing. Tour organizers seem to think that the thrilling early-summer drive through Wisconsin might be the perfect Father's day gift as opposed to, say, another ugly tie. So they've included a kind of money-back guarantee. Make that an "ugly tie" guarantee: "We guarantee that if the tour is given as a gift and your Dad complains that it wasn't all he thought it would be, we'll give him an ugly tie," McDonell said. "But we've never had a complaint yet."

You were wondering how the world's first auto race ended up being run in Wisconsin? A strange series of events conjured up this trivia-question masterpiece, a real piece of Americana based on State of Wisconsin Historical Society records and interviews with family descendants.

In 1873 an outbreak of equine distemper hit most horses in the Dairy State. That was a big blow to a region that depended on horsepower—and lots of it—to keep the wheels of commerce and agriculture turning. And the resultant work stoppage was a disaster.

The state legislature got an idea of how to possibly solve their problems and add to the progress of technology: they established a $10,000 prize—a huge sum in those times—to be awarded to anyone who could design a mechanized substitute for horses that could win a race of 200 miles from Green Bay to Madison.

To the cries of "Show me the money!" (well . . . maybe not), six vehicles eventually were developed for the road run. But only two of them steamed to the starting line on July 17, 1878. The "Oshkosh" and the "Green Bay" chugged through the Fox Cities toward Madison amid clouds of dust, crowds full of cheer, and cows so startled they may have made that jump over the moon.

Only the "Oshkosh" made it to the finish line in Madison,

taking 33 hours and 27 minutes for the 201-mile road trip, an average speed of 6 mph. Alexander Gallinger, who built the "Oshkosh," rightfully claimed the $10,000 purse.

Remember, however, that state legislatures, like most legislative bodies, are composed of many lawyers. So the legislature told Gallinger that they "expected better," a vehicle that was tougher and faster, and offered him only $5,000. Gallinger told the lawmakers to keep their money (he actually used more colorful language), and his "Oshkosh" steamed back home.

Topless Summer Touring

Why not get a little crazy and wander topless around the Badger State—as part of the annual Wisconsin Convertible Classic (WCC), held in mid-August. Starting in Madison, a caravan of open-air automobiles of all shapes, sizes, and ages leaves on a grand tour that winds over some of the most spectacularly scenic segments of the Great River Road edging the Mississippi River in the western portion of the state.

Another creation by lifelong, ragtop enthusiasts Gary Knowles (1961 Buick Electra) and Alex McDonnell (1976 "final edition" fuel-injected Cadillac Eldorado), the convertible caravan draws hundreds of open-top owners from all four corners of the country—and even as far away as Japan.

All you need to join the noncompetitive, family-oriented tour is a ragtop of any vintage. Past classics have included everything from 1934 Cords and a pink, "Elvis" 1963 Cadillac to Mazda Miatas and Chevy Geos. Even an ancient Austin Healy, pulled from beneath a corn crib, found its way into the lineup.

"There are no bad convertibles," says organizer Knowles. The WCC starts Thursday in Madison with a photo session and twilight cruising before beginning its run to the river. On Friday it rolls through Spring Green and the Wisconsin River Valley before reaching Prairie du Chien and the Great River Road. Saturday's leg of the tour explores the northern loop of the GRR, with glimpses of turkey vultures, prehistoric hillside rock outcroppings, and a river valley sometimes called the "American Rhine." It also includes forays into Minnesota (for more extraordinary views of Wisconsin from across the Mississippi), before winding up Sunday in LaCrosse.

Meals and accommodations are not included in the entry fee. But designated WCC hotels offer special-event rates to participants. Other fun doings during the tour include parties, car rallies, river cruises, prizes, T-shirts, and more.

For More Information

For information about these cool car classics, contact tour director Gary Knowles, 608-231-3884; call the tour hotline at 608-271-1335; or send E-mail requests to openair@ aol.com.

25

Lumberjack Legacy

HAYWARD

AT THE TURN OF THE CENTURY, HAYWARD WAS ONE OF THE rowdiest and wildest logging towns in the North Woods. The melody of a six-foot bucksaw and the jingle of the yoke chains of teams of oxen hauling downed timber out of wilderness forests was the music that lumberjacks made.

Today Hayward is a bustling resort town, with hundreds of nearby lakes and the Chequamegon National Forest offering all kinds of fishing, hiking, and biking adventures.

But for three days each summer (the last full weekend in July), Hayward turns back the clock to the days when burly lumberjacks ruled the woods. That's when it hosts the Lumberjack World Championships, with 200 of the top competitive timbermen from the United States and Canada (and as far away as Great Britain, New Zealand, Tasmania, and Australia) competing for thousands of dollars in prizes—the largest payout for any lumberjack event in the world.

This annual timberfest, nearly four decades old, originated from the everyday lumberjack work and play of the 1800s. That's when logging camps across North America would send their most skilled lumberjacks to engage in fierce competitions to determine who was "King of the Forest."

Muscular lumbermen now compete in one- and two-man bucksawing, power sawing, a variety of chopping events, logrolling, and speed climbing. All competitions take place in the Lumberjack Bowl, a large bay of Lake Hayward. It is a historic site, once used as a giant holding pond for the North Wisconsin Lumber Company.

Semipro events are held on Friday and Saturday mornings. Amateur logrolling (kids ages 3 to 17) is also slated for morning competitions, and there's a master's division for lumberjacks aged 50 and older.

However, the main events remain professional competitions, which begin early each afternoon. Thrill to speed climbing, when lumberjacks must scramble up a 90-foot-high fir spar pole and drop back to the ground in less than 30 seconds. Watch monstrous muscles twitch during sawing competitions when burly loggers grind through a 20-inch white-pine log in less than 10 seconds. Or listen to the chink of cold steel sinking into wood when competitors must chop through a 14-inch log in about 20 seconds.

Another favorite is the logrolling contest. Birlers go face-to-face atop a 12-foot-long cedar log, 15 inches in diameter, floating in the bay. First one to fall into the water loses. As the competition continues, logs get smaller and smaller, calling for increased skills. Eventually, the champion must remain high and dry while balancing atop a log only 12 inches in diameter.

If you can't make the World Championships, head to Hayward anytime from mid-June through early September for Scheer's Lumberjack Shows, located one mile east of Hayward on County B. Not only will you see action-packed lumberjack contests like canoe jousting, chopping, sawing, speed climbing, and logrolling, but you can attend "Lumberjack Show Outdoor Barbecues" and visit six Lumberjack Village specialty shops featuring North Woods souvenirs. For show days and times, call 715-634-5010.

Also nearby is Historyland Logging Camp, which offers logging camp museum tours and all-you-can-eat, family-style lumberjack breakfasts. Count on scrambled eggs lumberjack style; lumberjack American fries; French toast and pancakes; biscuits and muffins; homemade cinnamon bread; giant lumberjack donuts; apple juice, milk, and coffee. It's all served daily. For reservations call 800-255-5937 or 715-634-2579.

For More Information

General admission and reserved seating tickets are available for the Lumberjack World Championships; special three-day passes are also available, as well as senior's and children's discounts. Shows proceed rain or shine—there are no refunds. For more information, contact Lumberjack World Championships Foundation, P.O. Box 666, Hayward, WI 54843, 715-634-2484; Hayward Chamber of Commerce, 125 West First Street, State 27 and U.S. 63, P.O. Box 726, Hayward, WI 54843, 715-634-8662.

Lumberjack Legacy

26

Manitowoc Maritime Museum

MANITOWOC

STEPPING ABOARD THE USS *COBIA*, A WORLD WAR II SUBMA-rine that sank 13 enemy vessels in the Pacific, I felt an eerie chill. It wasn't just the excitement of being on a warship; what shocked me was the ship's incredibly claustrophobic quarters and the thought of 80 crew members jammed into the cigar-shaped sliver of steel on long, dangerous sea patrols. I didn't expect such drama during a visit to the downtown Manitowoc Maritime Museum.

This region is Wisconsin's historic maritime capital, whose natural bay and harbor made it an important ship-building site through World War II. Clipper ships were hammered together here in great numbers during the 1860s and 1870s. Then, beginning in 1939, shipbuilders concentrated on warships, producing 28 submarines for the navy (25 saw action, 4 were sunk), along with scores of minesweepers, sub chasers, and landing craft transports (LCTs).

The museum's "Harbors" exhibit explains various stages of the Manitowoc port development. An audiotape of crashing waves, foghorns, and screeching gulls sets the room's ambience as visitors walk through displays of early sailing vessels and steamships, artifacts, and historic harbor photographs. Most fascinating is a full-scale, room-size midship cross-section of the ship *Clipper City* as it appeared during construction in 1854. Designed as a lumber vessel, its most frequent run was Chicago to Milwaukee, some 90 nautical miles covered in five hours—that's about 18 knots.

Another terrific display highlights the *Christopher Columbus*, the only passenger whaleback (cigar-shaped hull) steamer ever built. It ferried more than two million passengers during Chicago's Columbian Exposition in 1893.

Manitowoc–Two Rivers also is the center of a large charter fishing fleet. More than 30 charter skippers offer half-day and full-day adventures, angling for fighters like lake trout, and coho salmon. (They'll also clean and freeze your catch.)

You can even fall asleep while listening to the waves crash against the shore by overnighting at the Inn on Maritime Bay, a hotel with nautical themes located on the harbor, next to the marina and just about one block from the Maritime Museum. It's also a short walk to the city's lakefront park, where you can watch great sunrises.

Finally, the only way to top this mini-seafaring adventure is by visiting during the town's annual Maritime Days, a three-day fest held in mid-August. Events include trout boils, water-ski exhibitions, a Venetian Night boat parade, a Coast Guard station open house, and tours aboard one of their sleek cutters.

FOR MORE INFORMATION

For information contact the Manitowoc Maritime Museum, 75 Maritime Drive, Manitowoc, WI 54221, 920-684-0218; for lists of charter fishing operations and other Manitowoc area information, contact the Manitowoc Chamber of Commerce, 1515 Memorial Drive, Manitowoc, WI 54221, 800-262-7892.

Summer

27

Wisconsin Golf

As any weekend wanderer soon discovers, there is much more to Wisconsin than dairy farms, cheese shops, and brat stops. But would you believe a golfer's paradise?

Don't take my word for it. Listen to Andy North, two-time champion of the prestigious U.S. Open and winner of more than $1,000,000 in lifetime earnings on the PGA tour.

"Golfers don't really know how good they've got it here in Wisconsin," says North, a Madison native. "Our courses are better than most anywhere else in the country."

You can find out for yourself by playing a few of the state's top links, and with several premier courses part of resort getaways, even nonplaying spouses or friends can have a weekend full of fun while you're puttering around.

SentryWorld, in Stevens Point, is an awesome course designed by renowned golf architect Robert Trent Jones. The 6,811-yard, par-72 gem is one of the few touring pro–caliber courses open daily to everyone from weekend duffers to top PGA hotshots. What distinguishes SentryWorld are sinister bogs, half-acre traps, ball-hungry lakes, five acres of flower-bed hazards, and multitiered greens that resemble ski hills.

Jones described SentryWorld as "very possibly my Mona Lisa" among his course designs. That means 35 acres of spring-fed lakes, large boulders framing fairways and greens, huge stands of birch and pine trees, and 83 maddening sand traps that total four acres.

SentryWorld's signature hole is number six, the 156-yard "Flower Hole" that generates so much publicity. Sand traps and more than 100,000 flowering plants surrounding a small island green create the most gorgeous golf hazard ever fashioned. Balls landing among rainbow colors cannot be retrieved; errant shooters must drop another ball on the side. So forget your sand wedge and bring some garden shears. For greens fees, car rental, and other information, call 715-345-1600.

Lawsonia, in Green Lake, has been rated by *Golf Digest* as one of the top public courses in America. The Links course is built in the tradition of Scottish courses—wide open and not too long, with little water and few trees. It, too, requires precision shots because of 91 sand traps and sprawling steepfaced bunkers. Elevated greens can display crazy undulations that sometimes make even short putts real adventures. Its 71.5 rating is the highest of any Wisconsin public course.

However, the Green Lake area offers 72 holes of golf on four distinctly different courses. A great way to take advantage of this variety is by signing up for one of the area's lodging and golf packages. One of the best is Heidel House Resort, located on the shore of Wisconsin's deepest lake. It offers 200 guest rooms, suites, and cottages, indoor and outdoor swimming pools, a fitness center, water sports, tennis courts, hiking trails, paddleboats, good food, live entertainment, and more. For golf package information, call 800-444-2812.

The Americana Resort, in Lake Geneva, boasts two of the state's most distinguished courses. The Briar Patch, designed by golf architect Pete Dye and legendary pro Jack Nicklaus, measures 6,700 yards of pure torture. It is also a Scottish-style course having little water, few trees, and small greens—a test of "target golf," with narrow fairways lined

Summer

by knee-high heather and deep, natural rough. An errant shot almost automatically penalizes a player; even if you find the ball, an iron shot out of this stuff is almost impossible.

For a completely different experience, wrestle "The Brute," Americana's other course—an incredible 7,258 yards with open fairways and greens guarded by water, rolling hills, and more than 70 bunkers. But the real story of the Brute is its greens—huge, manicured carpets claiming to be among the largest in the world, averaging 10,000 square feet each. At one of the "double-greens," used for tandem holes, it's nothing to find yourself left with nearly a 100-foot putt. The sprawling resort also offers swimming pools, a fitness center, fine dining, and live entertainment. For golf package information call 414-248-8811 or 800-558-3417.

The "beauty of these beasts" remains Blackwolf Run, in Kohler. Gem of the luxurious American Club resort flaunting European elegance, gourmet-style food, a "Sports Core" with all kinds of athletic facilities, and a private 500-acre wilderness retreat for hiking, hunting, and fishing, the course has been lavishly praised by almost all golf publications.

Named "Best New Public Golf Course" upon its opening in 1988, the Pete Dye–designed 36-hole layout has tremendous variety. It is target golf at its finest, offering British-style links challenges with pot bunkers, steep mounding, tall rough, and high plateau greens. The Sheboygan River randomly meanders through the course, creating a wonderland environment. "There could not be a better natural setting for golf," Dye said. Call 800-344-2838 for information.

FOR MORE INFORMATION

For a list and addresses of the above and other state golf courses, Wisconsin Tourism Development, P.O. Box 7606, Madison, WI 53707, 608-266-2161 or 800-372-2737.

28

The Wild Side of Door County

IF YOU WANT ACTION IN PARADISE, HEAD TO DOOR COUNTY'S western shore, which edges the blue waters of Green Bay. A haven for artists, writers, and craftspeople, it remains one of the Midwest's top weekend getaway havens.

Galleries, museums, boutiques, and specialty shops line streets of picturesque lakeside towns offering fabulous harbor views. Fine-sand beaches offer splashy fun. Quaint country inns pamper guests. And restaurants serve such Door County specialties as thin Swedish pancakes dappled with lingonberries or boiled whitefish.

One word of warning: Sometimes it seems the entire Midwest is here at the same time—especially on summer weekends that find State 42 almost blockaded by wall-to-wall traffic, parking spaces sparse, and restaurant waiting lists that leave you sitting around for more than an hour.

Just remember that off-season adventurers (early spring, late fall) can have the Door almost to themselves if they don't mind cooler, rainy weather. Whatever your choice, here are some of the wild-side highlights on this thumb-shaped 70-mile-long peninsula separating the warm, tranquil waters of Green Bay from the cold, wild waves of Lake Michigan.

Sturgeon Bay is the starting point for any Door County ramble. The county seat continues to be a major Great Lakes shipbuilding center. Stop at the Door County Maritime Museum (at the foot of Florida Street) to see historic boats from the 1900s and a turn-of-the-century pilothouse. Call 920-743-8139.

Downtown offers some fine art galleries and folk art boutiques. In the heart of the action is the Inn at Cedar Crossing (336 Louisiana Street), a historic bed-and-breakfast hostelry with elegant antiques, fireplaces, and whirlpools; call 920-743-4200. The White Lace Inn (16 North Fifth Avenue) is one of the most romantic in the Midwest; call 920-743-1105. For artsy types, the Hillside Orchard Retreat offers loom-and-spinning classes, screen-writing courses and acting classes with bay views on its 100-acre spread. Call 920-743-9160.

Egg Harbor, sitting on a bluff overlooking Green Bay, offers a little bit of everything, but its main claim to fame is the Birch Creek Music Center, a nationally acclaimed summer arts academy where talented students perform evening summer concerts in a pristine setting; for its concert series schedule, call 920-868-3763.

Fish Creek is the soul of Door County. It's home to the Peninsula Players (the oldest summer theater in America), the Peninsula Music Festival, the American Folklore Theater, the Peninsula Art School, the Peninsula Arts Theater, and more. It has more of the county's fine-arts shops, boutiques, and galleries than any other village. You can rent bicycles for spins around the town or charter a boat for bay cruises.

Fish Creek also claims what's been called "the jewel of the Wisconsin State Park system"—Peninsula State Park,

Summer

with 3,700 acres of woodlands, a great beach, golf course, hiking trails, and towering limestone bluffs that crash nearly 200 feet down to the blue waters of Green Bay.

Let's not forget the White Gull Inn, home to the county's most lavishly produced "fish boil." This must-see is a Scandinavian ritual combining whitefish steaks, potatoes, and onions in a huge boiling cauldron over an open fire. Get your cameras ready for the "final boil"—when a secret ingredient is added, causing a rush of fiery flames to lick the sky. Call 920-868-3517.

Ephraim is the most picturesque village in the entire peninsula. Nestled on the shores of Eagle Harbor, its turn-of-the-century ambience includes charming hostelries (the Ephraim Inn offers the best harbor views; call 920-854-4515); a famous ice cream parlor (Wilson's, 9990 Water Street, State 42); and the largest windsurfing outfitter on the peninsula (Windsurf Door County, 9876 Water Street).

Sister Bay is noted for its Scandinavian hospitality. To experience just that, head to Al Johnson Swedish Restaurant and Butik, housed in a Norwegian-made dark wood building with goats grazing on its grass-covered roof. Its claim to fame is paper-thin Swedish pancakes served with tangy lingonberries. There's also a fine boutique sporting Scandinavian imports. Call 920-854-2626.

Ellison Bay boasts one of the finest scenic vistas on the Door—a 200-foot crest (near the Grand View Motel) that "guards" the road into town. Also noteworthy is the Clearing, located north of town. Set on 128 acres tilted high above the waters of Green Bay, this rural school offers more than 40 adult courses in art, literature, painting, music, and crafts. Call 920-854-4088.

Gills Rock is known as the "top o' the thumb" for its northernmost position on the tip of the peninsula. Its commerical fishing industry is always good for colorful photos at daybreak and sunset (when boats leave and return to the

The Wild Side of Door County

municipal docks). Stores offer maritime crafts and knick-knacks. The Shoreline Resort sells some of the best sandwiches you can find on the Door, and they don't cost a car payment. You can also charter a fishing boat for salmon, rainbow trout, and coho adventures.

Washington Island is reached by ferryboat from Gills Rock and Northport. You'll have to cross "Death's Door" to get there, a rowdy strait that claimed many ships back in the clipper-ship era. The island itself is famed as the oldest Icelandic settlement in the United States. The best way to explore is by hopping aboard the Viking Tour Train, which whisks visitors on 90-minute guided tours to spots like Den Norsk Grenda, Schoolhouse Beach, and the Art & Nature Center. Call 920-854-2972.

If you prefer, rent a bike or moped and explore the island on your own: see rolling farmlands, dense forests, and white sand beaches dotted by tall sand dunes sweeping down to the turbulent waters of Lake Michigan.

FOR MORE INFORMATION

Door County annual events stretch throughout the year. Some highlights are Sister Bay's Winterfest, in January; Fish Creek Winter Games, in February; the June Jubilee and the Door County Maritime Festival in August (both in Sturgeon Bay); Newport Wilderness Day, in Ellison Bay; and Sturgeon Bay's November Christmas Walk. For more information, contact Door County Chamber of Commerce, P.O. Box 406, Sturgeon Bay, WI 54235, 920-743-4456; Washington Island Chamber of Commerce, Washington Island, WI 54246, 920-847-2225.

29

German Fest

MILWAUKEE

YOU CAN BUY A BRATWURST AT A BREWERS GAME, CHOW down on sauerkraut and sausage at a German beer hall near the Bradley Center before a Bucks game, or join the numbers of evening revelers who have their choice among 34 German clubs strung throughout the city. It's not surprising in a town like Milwaukee, with 52 percent of its population claiming German ancestry, the largest single concentration in any U.S. metropolitan area of any one ethnic group. So you'd expect Milwaukee to celebrate its dominant oompah heritage in a big way.

Jawohl!

It's simply called German Fest, an annual midsummer weekend-long party held at Maier Festival Park on Lake Michigan. It is the largest German festival in North America.

Every year more than 100,000 people from around the United States and Europe converge on this city for a slice of *gemütlichkeit*, not to mention schnitzel, *Spanferkel*, sauerbraten, and strudel. And the weekend's Bavarian bash packs even more Teutonic punch into its eclectic schedule, with everything from Wagner and Beethoven selections performed by the New German Fest Symphony Orchestra to wiener-dog races.

Anyone slightly familiar with Oktoberfest or other German party times, knows that music plays a huge role in the celebration. Every day at German Fest, nine stages provide continuous entertainment from noon to midnight, with both local performers and premier groups from Austria and Germany providing the tunes.

In the past, fest musical coups have even included a rare United States appearance by the Erdinger Musikanten, official house band of the world-famous Hofbräu Haus, in Munich. Who knows what surprises await revelers this year?

Other bands and musical entertainers come from Austria, Bavaria, and German ethnic-enclaves in the United States. Special tune times daily include "Battle of the Bands" at the Gemutlichkeit Tent; Vienna Strings at the Wine Stage; and traditional oompah at the Beer Garden.

Summer

Classical music fans aren't forgotten, with appearances by the New German Fest Symphony Orchestra, composed of 75 musicians mostly from the Milwaukee Symphony Orchestra. Tickets to this show include admission to the German Fest. Call 414-464-9749 or any Ticket Master outlet.

More highlights include the following:

- Saturday afternoon's German Fest parade featuring 70 marching bands, ethnic dancers, and colorful costumes

- *Trachtenschau*, an elaborate display of ethnic fashions from Germany, Austria, and Switzerland

- Yodeling shows featuring master yodelers from Bavaria and audience-participation contests

- *Marktplatz*, with authentic European crafts, including demonstrations by master wood-carvers from Germany

- A culture tent offering genealogy assistance, German travel videos, a German language center, a bookstore with fairy-tale display, and more handmade German crafts

- Displays of M. I. Hummel ceramic collector figurines, including demonstrations by a Hummel master painter

- Nightly fireworks shows

There's also plenty of kids' stuff. Children can learn German folk dances, make their own Bavarian arts and crafts, see magicians, listen to singers, boot a ball during a "soccer kick" with Milwaukee's pro soccer team, see live theater shows, listen to the all-children "Kinderchor," and more.

A new German Fest craze debuted in 1992 and continues to be a crowd favorite: wiener-dog racing. That's right, more than 20 of the longest, wiggliest weiner dogs (provided by a local dachshund club) squeeze through an obstacle course of tunnels, hurdles, and water hazards during the Dachshund Derby on Sunday afternoon at the sports area. Marvel at the silliness when pooches are gussied up for a costume parade, portraying everyone from Wilhelm Tell to Carmen Miranda.

FOR MORE INFORMATION

Admission is charged, with children under 12 admitted free when accompanied by an adult. Ticket prices include admission to all exhibits and entertainment except the Marcus Amphitheater's classical music concerts. Maier Festival Park is located less than one mile off I-94 in Milwaukee (take I-794 east to the lakefront and follow the Summerfest smile signs to the park). For additional information contact German Fest, 8229 West Capitol Drive, Milwaukee, WI 53222, 414-464-9444.

30

Badger Car Ferry

MANITOWOC TO LUDINGTON, MICHIGAN

HOW WOULD YOU LIKE TO TAKE A RELAXING OCEAN CRUISE IN Wisconsin? Just one small problem, you say. An ocean?

Well, don't let a little technicality like that stop you from having the time of your life. Just hop aboard the *Badger*, once an old bucket of a car ferry that's plied a course across Lake Michigan between Manitowoc, Wisconsin, and Ludington, Michigan, on and off for a few decades. Now it has been transformed into a people-oriented boat, still ferrying cars across the waves, but with much more comfort and conveniences for its passengers.

Let's set the record straight. The *Badger* is still a hulk of a ship—a looming black-and-white metal leviathan whose superstructure stands 410 feet high and 60 feet across at the beam. It can carry 520 passengers and 120 vehicles, including cars, trucks, and recreational vehicles.

But it's a kinder and gentler experience than it used to be.

To best simulate a languid ocean cruise, try the 10-hour round-trip sail. You can reserve a stateroom for rest and privacy; there are comfortable lounges, cocktail bars, a buffet restaurant, and movie rooms. Kids can wander the onboard museum or video arcade. I like to grab a chair and bask in the glory of a lake crossing.

One shrill blast of the ship's whistle signals its shove-off from port. The tall smokestack billows clouds of black smoke and the boat shudders; it's the same vibration you'll feel throughout the cruise. But you get used to it rather quickly, and it almost becomes reassuring, like the rocking of a Pullman car over steel rails.

The upper lounge's buffet lunch includes staples like barley soup, salad, meat loaf, barbecued pork, vegetables, and rice; the menu changes daily. After a bite, head up to the deck to enjoy the journey.

Whitecaps break across the green-blue water on this magnificent inland sea. Gulls squawk overhead, occasionally skimming the water on their own lunch break, hoping to snare a fish. Breathe in the fresh air and relax. Let the sun soak into your bones and the wind whip through your soul.

The ride can be very smooth. Usual top speed is 18 mph; the *Badger* can reach 24 mph. However, unruly weather and brisk winds can stir up quite a tempest. When heavy rollers dominate, the captain steers the boat along a course that's least likely to discomfort his passengers.

You'll also probably see quite a bit of traffic on the lake. It can be fascinating to watch modern cargo ships, technological wonders longer than a football field, sail silently by without evidence of a single soul aboard.

The gentle rolling waves can induce an almost trancelike tranquility. But the moment is shattered by another shrill blast of the whistle signaling the *Badger*'s arrival at Ludington, the ferry's eastern terminus. If you're cruising round-trip, you have about two hours to explore.

The Ludington area is a wonder of sparkling shoreline backed by tall pines. Downtown's Ludington Avenue is annually decorated with more than 50,000 petunias. Hop aboard shiny red double-decker buses to visit either Ludington State Park, with more great lake vistas, or White Pine Village, a turn-of-the-century living-history museum with more than 20 historic buildings.

FOR MORE INFORMATION

The *Badger* departs Ludington, Michigan, daily (eastern time) in early morning and departs Manitowoc daily (central time) in early afternoon. Beginning in late June, late-evening cruises are added. The season ends mid-October. One-way, round-trip, reserved stateroom, vehicle, and bicycle fares are charged. For more information, contact Lake Michigan Car Ferry Service, P.O. Box 708, Ludington, MI 49431, 800-841-4243.

31

Europe in Wisconsin

NEW GLARUS AND MOUNT HOREB

FORGET ABOUT OUTRAGEOUS CONTINENTAL HOTEL RATES, expensive airfare and long trans-Atlantic flights that end in jetlag.

Traveling to "Europe" this summer should take no longer than a scenic drive into Wisconsin. And the best time to go is when its hills come alive with the sound of music during two of the state's most popular ethnic celebrations—the Heidi Festival, slated for the last weekend of June, in New Glarus; and the Song of Norway Festival, on weekends from the end of June through July, in Mount Horeb.

New Glarus's Heidi Festival is this charming Swiss colony's best summer-season bash. The Swiss of New Glarus maintain close connections with the canton of Glarus in Switzerland by preserving the customs and rich traditions of the Old World. Visitors see several styles of chalets around town, and many people maintain the Swiss custom of painting the name of their occupation on their home's facade.

You can taste tempting samples of *Kalberwurst* and *Land-jaegger* at sausage shops that follow Old World recipes, walk to the *Schoco-Laden* (chocolate shop) for sweet Swiss confections, marvel at fine wood carvings (for which the Swiss are renowned) and other imported handmade crafts, or sip a frothy Glarner *Bier* over oompah music from a balcony table overlooking picturesque downtown at the New Glarus Hotel, a favorite spot for visitors. And let's not forget the Swiss cheese shops.

A few years ago, I passed through Switzerland's canton of Glarus and was struck by the similarity between that region's rolling green hills and this Wisconsin landscape tamed by Swiss immigrants in 1845. It is that spirit and heritage, complete with Swiss flags, colorful costumes, folk dancing, yodeling, music, and other ethnic folk arts, that the Heidi festival salutes.

The centerpiece event is the drama *Heidi*, based on Johanna Spyri's story about an orphaned Swiss girl and her love for her gruff grandfather and his home in the Alps. The heartwarming tale, staged by local amateurs at the town's high school, is an enduring summer treat. Reserved and general admission tickets are available.

Summer

Also part of the weekend's festivities are the Little Switzerland Festival, a musical celebration with dancing, yodeling, *Thalerschwingen*, and flag throwing; and the Heidi Craft and Food Fair, featuring Swiss lace, embroidery, ethnic foods, and more.

The other major ethnic bash in New Glarus is the Wilhelm Tell Festival, held over September's Labor Day weekend. The story of the famed archer includes productions in both English and German. Also featured are Swiss music, yodeling, alpenhorns, folk dancing, and songs.

The Norwegian settlement of Mount Horeb, about 15 miles west of New Glarus, can trace its Song of Norway Festival back to midsummer's eve celebrations in Norway. It is a smorgasbord of music, drama, and dance, with ethnic food and crafts adding to the fun.

Located in the state's Blue Mound region (highest elevation in southern Wisconsin), with steep-sided valleys often guarded by trolls (good-luck elves, according to locals),

Mount Horeb has much to offer visitors. More than 80 arts, crafts, and antique dealers feature imported Norwegian linens, porcelain, and jewelry.

Nearby is Little Norway (called *Nissedahle*—Valley of the Elves), a Norwegian outdoor museum that is part of an immigrant Norwegian homestead settled in 1856. Costumed guides take visitors through historic buildings filled with authentic pioneer Norwegian furnishings. You'll also see my favorite, the Norway Building; it's a re-created 12th-century *stavekirke* (church), ornately decorated with handcrafted gingerbread, that houses the museum's collection of antique Norwegian wood carvings and silver. The building was constructed in Norway by that country's government and used at the 1893 Chicago Columbian Exposition.

Make sure you see the Hauge Lutheran Church, just a few miles down the road. Off the tourist path, it's a small log church built by Norwegian settlers and preserved by their descendants.

Performances of *The Song of Norway* take place at the outdoor stage on the grounds of Cave of the Mounds, four miles west of town. The play is an adaptation of the long-running Broadway musical that weaves tunes of famed Norwegian composer Edvard Grieg through a highly romantic (and fictionalized) account of his life. The Norwegian folk costumes and ballroom gowns are spectacular; music is provided by a 26-piece orchestra. Advance and gate tickets are available; kids pay half-price.

Europe in Wisconsin

For More Information

Contact New Glarus Chamber of Commerce, P.O. Box 713, New Glarus, WI 53574, 608-527-2095; Mount Horeb Chamber of Commerce, P.O. Box 84, Mount Horeb, WI 53572, 608-437-5914; Song of Norway Festival, 608-437-4600.

Fall

32

Fabulous Fall Colors

WITH FORESTS COVERING APPROXIMATELY 40 PERCENT OF THE state, Wisconsin is a paradise of autumn hues for fall color hounds. Millions of acres of woodlands erupt in fiery scarlets, coppers, bright oranges, and shiny golds throughout the state. And the color season, spanning the windswept rocky coastlines of Lake Superior in the north all the way down to snug hidden valleys in the south, can last from six to eight beautiful weeks.

Peak color usually hits in mid-October, depending on weather and location. Mother Nature requires warm sunny days, cool nights, and adequate moisture for her best colorama show. Of course, an early frost can put an end to the whole thing before it even gets started. Trees also start turning a week or two earlier in the colder north than in the southern part of the state. If you start in the north and work your way down, you can extend the season and see the best colors in all parts of the state.

Perhaps there's no better way to enjoy the Badger state's color caravan than by driving its back roads, considered among the best maintained in the nation. Here are some suggestions for a weekend of wild hues.

North Woods

If you can't find color in lumberjack country, where sprawling forests dominate the landscape, you're just not trying. One of the best color drives is State 77, designated as the state's first National Scenic Byway. The road stretches 29 miles through Chequamegon National Forest between Hayward and Glidden in the northwest portion of the state.

Another color hot spot is Land O' Lakes on U.S. 45, just before the Michigan border in north-central Wisconsin. Slices of Vilas County Roads B and C offer "tunnels of color," where you literally drive your car through a corridor of autumn hues. Or take a ride on the lake itself, surrounded by tall forests bursting with an artist's palette of colors.

Fall

Lake Superior Shoreline

State 13 meanders along Lake Superior's craggy coastline for about 90 miles between South Range and Ashland. Make a stop in the little town of Cornucopia to visit its elaborate Russian-Orthodox church. You can wander the historic fishing village of Bayfield or take a ferryboat to the Apostle Islands, a nationally protected archipelago that's a color paradise in its own right (see Chapter 15).

Door County

This narrow peninsula, part of the state's "thumb" that juts out into Lake Michigan, has been called the Cape Cod of the Midwest. It boasts more miles of shoreline, more state parks, and more lighthouses than any other county in the United States. Road warriors will marvel at color-splashed trees standing atop limestone bluffs and towering over rocky shores and sandy beaches. Drive through the peninsula's interior farms and woodlands for even more spectacular color views. The western shore, along Green Bay, is dotted with picturesque fishing villages, artists' galleries, boutiques, country inns, and unique restaurants. Don't miss the traditional Door County fish boil, an illuminating way to prepare whitefish and potatoes.

The Kettle Moraine

The last great glacier of more than 10,000 years ago sculpted a miles-long gouge of landforms with strange names like *kettles*, *kames*, *eskers*, and *drumlins*. See them at the Henry Reuss Ice Age Visitor Center, in Campbellsport (the Kettle Moraine State Forest northern unit), for exhibits on glacial history and for their spectacular fall colors. Also climb the Parnell Tower, located off County A about four miles south of Greenbush, whose observation platform offers a sensational panoramic vista of surrounding forests.

Another place from which to take in the views of Kettle color is the overlook at Holy Hill Shrine, in Hubertus, off State 167 (halfway between the Kettle Moraine State Forest's northern and southern units).

In the southern unit (near Eagle), colors explode at Old World Wisconsin (located on State 67; see Chapter 20), a living-history museum featuring restored homesteads of the state's immigrant pioneers. And the Kettle Moraine Scenic Steam Train, in North Lake off State 83, chugs for an eight-mile round-trip through color-tinged woodlands.

Southern Wisconsin

The Swiss village of New Glarus (see Chapter 31) is a little piece of Europe tucked into the gently rolling valleys of southern Wisconsin. Wander streets lined with traditional Swiss architecture, eat ethnic delicacies, and wash them down with an imported beer (Swiss, of course). A small museum highlights artifacts of its ethnic pioneers; town boutiques offer Swiss imports. Two places not to miss are the village's butcher and bakery shops.

Horicon Marsh National Wildlife Refuge, in Horicon, is home to 200,000 honking Canada geese who swoop down on the wetland every fall in their journey from summer breeding grounds in Canada's Hudson Bay to winter digs far south. Prime goose-watching time is mid-October; the best spot is from State 49, which slices through the northern portion of the marsh.

Fall

Great River Road

About 300 miles of ribboned road (mostly along State 35) parallel the Mississippi River, with 500-foot limestone bluffs studded with color-bursting foliage. Quaint river towns like Hudson offer splendid turn-of-the-century architecture. Cassville's 1800s living-history museum celebrates autumn harvest season each October. Wyalusing State Park features some of the finest vistas atop the bluffs lining the Mississippi. And there's a buffalo ranch near Midway that's one of the most successful operations of its kind in the country.

For More Information

For updated fall-color reports, call 800-372-2737; reports run mid-September through October. For other fall color touring information, contact Wisconsin Division of Tourism, P.O. Box 7970, Madison, WI 53707.

Fabulous Fall Colors

33

Door County's Quiet Side

EASTERN SHORE

A THICK FOG ROLLED IN OFF LAKE MICHIGAN, SHROUDING everything more than 10 feet away in nature's misty curtain. Our girls, Kate and Dayne, squealed with delight as they ran ahead of their parents and grandparents, disappearing into the soupy mist as we followed a path along the shore in Whitefish Dunes State Park. Whitecaps crashed against the sand, wind whipped across the beach, and voices could hardly be heard over Mother Nature's noisemaking. The dune-swept landscape is so breathtakingly isolated, so wild, so deserted that we could have been walking some remote trail on Cape Cod.

But we were enjoying Door County's "quiet side." That's how residents refer to the 100-mile shoreline on the eastern side of the thumblike peninsula jutting into Lake Michigan. It's definitely not for everybody. Families looking for sunny, calm beaches for their kids should head to the Green Bay side of the Door, where sheltered harbors render lake waters tranquil. Over there the best spot for toddlers to early teens is Ephraim's public beach.

But lakeside temperatures are five to ten degrees cooler on the quiet side than on the bay side. Winds are stronger and more constant. Fog often obscures views and dampens hikers. Towns tend to be stark, homey, and unassuming, rather than the bustling array of hotels, inns, restaurants, art galleries, and condo complexes that lure the bulk of travelers to bayside resorts such as Fish Creek, Sister Bay, and Ephraim.

Yet for those who want to relax in peace or explore nature's rugged handiwork, the quiet side is a revelation. Here are highlights of our three-day visit to Door's quiet side.

Gills Rock, which is located at the top of the thumb, overlooks Porte des Mortes (Door of Death), the watery strait that separates Door County from Washington Island. The current tossed waters made this passage a shipwreck graveyard—hence the name given by French explorers more than 300 years ago. You can rent scuba gear and explore these wrecks or visit the local maritime museum.

We simply enjoyed the water view while lunching at the Shoreline Resort, still the best place on the Door for a tasty sandwich that won't cost a second mortgage.

A short ride south brings you to Newport State Park, a 2,400-acre semi-wilderness retreat once the site of a thriving logging village that was made up of more than 20 buildings as well as a long pier and loading dock reaching out into Lake Michigan.

Nature has reclaimed Newport, which offers 11 miles of rugged shoreline, 28 miles of marked hiking trails, and 175 species of birds. Especially popular are the interpretive programs. We liked the trail that led us to Europe Lake, whose warm, placid waters sharply contrast with the thundering surf of Lake Michigan, only a narrow isthmus away.

Quiet Rowley Bay, just south of Newport, provides ways to explore the Door's natural wonders on both land and sea. Trek & Trail, a wilderness outfitter located on the outposts of the Wagon Trail Resort, offers sea kayaking on everything from quiet backwaters of the Mink River Sanctuary, itself teeming with wildlife, to the open expanses of the lake. Two-hour introductory courses and overnight and weekend excursions are available. You also can rent mountain bikes to explore overland wonders. Call 800-354-8735.

Perhaps the photographic highlight of the quiet side's treasures is Cana Island Lighthouse, located off County Road Q just north of Baileys Harbor. Built in 1869, the lighthouse is reached by walking across a rocky spit of land no more than 20 feet wide. In times of high water, this "trail" can be covered by more than three feet of wild water.

We learned that the rocks, which were indeed a graveyard for many 19th-century ships, still pose a threat to today's Great Lakes traffic. So the U.S. Coast Guard still operates the 89-foot-tall lighthouse, whose prism can be seen for 18 miles.

Also off County Q, just before reaching Baileys Harbor, is the Ridges Sanctuary, one of America's largest wildflower preserves. Miles of hiking trails loop through this 1,000-acre wonderland that includes two historic U.S. Lighthouse Service range lights, and more than 25 native orchids.

Be sure to wear proper dress for serious hiking (long shirt, long pants, hiking boots) and stay on marked paths since poison ivy grows along many trail edges, especially near the parking lot. Hours are daily; call 414-839-2802.

About halfway down the quiet side is Baileys Harbor, Door's original county seat. It's another tranquil refuge from the bayside hustle, with a few specialty stores located "downtown" right on Lake Michigan. Baileys is also known for its charter fishing fleet, with half-day and full-day trips pursuing record chinook salmon, steelhead, and brown trout. Call 800-345-5253.

Jacksonport's biggest claim to fame might be its location:

Door County's Quiet Side

exactly midway between the Equator and the North Pole. The town's Lakeside Park is among the most pleasant little beaches for kids, rivaled only by the more secluded Baileys Harbor public beach.

The area also has two shouldn't-miss natural wonders. Just south of town is Cave Point County Park, where the thundering surf crashes into wave-worn caves, carved from limestone cliffs with elemental force. And at Whitefish Dunes State Park, eight miles north of Sturgeon Bay, the largest sand dune in Wisconsin stands 93 feet above Lake Michigan. Call 414-823-2400.

FOR MORE INFORMATION

Fall

For mailing addresses and more information about the peninsula, contact the Door County Chamber of Commerce, P.O. Box 406, Sturgeon Bay, WI 54235, 800-527-3529 or 920-743-4456.

34

Horicon Marsh

HORICON

IT'S OCTOBER AT HORICON MARSH. FALL DAYS SHORTEN, THE air turns crisp, the landscape is brushed with autumn gold. And wedge after wedge of honking Canada geese drops noisily onto this wetland sanctuary, searching for food, water, and a resting spot on their long journey south. It's another fall flying spectacular, one of nature's longest-running shows.

From September to January each year, about 200,000 of the big black-necked birds drop by to sample goodies on this 32,000-acre marsh just 55 miles northwest of Milwaukee and protected by state and federal conservation agencies. It serves as the birds' main Midwest stopover point on their 1,000-mile journey from nesting grounds near Hudson Bay in Canada to wintering lands at the confluence of the Ohio and Mississippi Rivers.

Geese numbers usually peak around mid-October if the fall is crisp. An unusually warm autumn can mean an overwhelming number of Canadas on the marsh—as many as 300,000.

And let's not forget that more than 200 species of birds call the marsh home during parts of the year, including 23 kinds of ducks, whistling swans, sandhill cranes, and Foster's terns. Full-time residents include white-tailed deer, coyotes, red fox, skunk, raccoon, otter, opossum, and muskrats.

October is prime goose-watching time. The U.S. Fish and Wildlife Service runs a Horicon Visitor Information Center at State 49 and County Road Z (about six miles east of Waupun) providing goose watchers with a scenic overlook and free maps pinpointing top observation spots. The maps also detail "Wild Goose Parkway," a 30-mile-long road system marked with green signs that encircles the marsh. It can be very crowded here on weekends. Another information booth in downtown Horicon (Lake and Vine streets) is open weekends. Or you can get goose-watching news via radio broadcasts on 1610 AM.

One of the best goose-watching points is along State 49 (about three miles east of Waupun), which pierces the northern edge of the refuge. You can pull off the shoulder of the road and see thousands of Canadas from your car or get out and walk along six miles of marsh trails maintained by the U.S. Fish and Wildlife Service.

The Marsh Haven Nature Center is located just across the road, with an observation deck rising 30 feet above the marsh, allowing a great view of the birds. Naturalist-led wildlife programs are offered Sunday afternoons in October.

Horicon has other excellent foot trails, with two paths stretching about two miles each onto the marsh—one even has a long boardwalk where you can walk among the tall grasses and cattails. Yet any of the roads surrounding the marsh offers good opportunities to see plenty of geese. Be sure to explore (eyes only; it's private property) lands adjacent to the marsh since geese often tend to scatter when they're on the ground. This way you'll miss some of the

Fall

inevitable traffic tie-ups along more popular goose-viewing routes.

If you don't want to drive the marsh roads yourself, you can enjoy guided wetland tours. Fond du Lac, 12 miles north of Horicon, hosts an annual October celebration called "Spectacle of the Geese." It features seminars and lectures (often given by a Wisconsin Department of Natural Resources naturalist) explaining wetland history, annual migration of geese, and resource management. A two-hour guided bus tour follows.

A number of Fond du Lac restaurants offer fall harvest dinners throughout October, featuring champagne-roasted pheasant, roast duck with raspberry sauce, duck with cherry-brandy glaze, wild rice, squash, homemade breads, and desserts.

Another option is Blue Heron Tours, which conducts boat excursions on the marsh. In October, boat tours are offered only Saturdays and Sundays. For about 25 years, Marc Zuelsdorf and his family have taken visitors on one-hour "nature studies" using 30-foot pontoon boats. Tours meet at the Blue Heron landing on State Highway 33 in downtown Horicon (near the bridge). Blue Heron also rents canoes to paddle around the marsh.

Marsh sunrises and sunsets—which are the best times to see black clouds of honking geese—can be quite cold. Be sure to wear a warm jacket and a good pair of waterproof hiking boots. Don't forget binoculars and a camera for some great nature shots, and a thermos of coffee or hot chocolate is a good idea for some added warmth.

Farms surrounding the marsh often have roadside stands selling homegrown vegetables and fresh produce. Look for eggs, country squash, pumpkins, apples, cider, and more. A recommended stop is Tom Dooley Orchards, near Waupun, which has some of the best homemade apple pie around these parts.

FOR MORE INFORMATION

In October Wisconsin's Department of Natural Resources offers weekend nature programs at its Horicon Headquarters on State 28, two miles north of Horicon. Towns surrounding the marsh celebrate with festivals, including Horicon's September "Autumn Art on the Marsh"; Beaver Dam's September "Colorfest"; Mayville's October "Audubon Days"; and Waupun's October "Wild Goose Days."

For more information, contact the U.S. Fish and Wildlife Service, Horicon National Wildlife Refuge, W4279 Headquarters Road, Mayville, WI 53050, 920-387-2658; Wisconsin Department of Natural Resources, Horicon Headquarters, N7725 Wisconsin Highway 28, Horicon, WI 53032, 920-387-7860; Horicon Chamber of Commerce, P.O. Box 23, Horicon, WI 53032, 920-485-3200; Blue Heron Tours, 101 Main Street, Horicon, WI 53032, 920-485-4663; Fond du Lac Convention and Visitors Bureau, 19 West Scott Street, Fond du Lac, WI 54935, 920-923-3010 or 800-937-9123; Tom Dooley Orchards, W5759 Wisconsin 49, Waupun, WI 53963, 920-324-3664.

Fall

35

Wisconsin Originals

A REALLY FUN WAY TO EXPLORE WISCONSIN IS BY TRACING THE story of its statehood—from the original Ojibwa warriors who once lived here and continuing on with the stories of the French voyageurs, miners, missionaries and ministers, sailors, industrialists, and thousands of immigrant farmers who have left their mark on the dairy state—as you take a look at a few of the Badger State's wackier paeans to its out-doorsman and iconoclastic roots.

Here are a few of those stories that make for great getaways.

Wa Swa Goning

Before the French explorers came to Wisconsin, Native Americans traversed its land of woods and waters. Among these peoples were the Ojibwa Indians (called Chippewa by European settlers), who were led by their chief Keesh Ke Mun ("Sharpened Stone") during the mid-1700s into north-central Wisconsin, the area we call Lac du Flambeau.

"Lake of the Flame" was so called by French voyageurs because the Ojibwa used torches to spear fish at night.

Today the region, site of the Lac du Flambeau Reservation, is home to some of the most historic and culturally significant displays of Indian ancestry in Wisconsin.

You might first visit the reservation's Ojibwa Museum and Cultural Center, where you'll see everything from 100-year-old dugout canoes and Native American arts and crafts to the reconstruction of a French fur-trading post. But the newest museum attraction is getting much of the attention: Wa Swa Goning, an authentic Ojibwa village nestled amid 20 pristine forest acres edging Moving Cloud Lake. You'll see a living history demonstration of daily chores performed by villagers, birchbark wigwams and handmade bows and arrows, canoes being handmade by native peoples, and other villagers working on Native American crafts.

For more information call 715-588-3303, ext. 261.

Curse of Bearskull Lake

Do you have enough courage to challenge the "Legend of Emerson Park," located on Highway 182 in Springstead? The guide tells us that an old Chippewa legend says that Bearskull Lake is sacred. "Any white man who has anything to do with the lake or its vicinity will have everlasting ill fortune."

Think that's an idle threat or a wizened tribal legend? Consider the story of the Emerson brothers, drawn to Bearskull Lake to harvest virgin timber in 1904 and using the wood to build the town of Emerson. That very town was destroyed by fire, then rebuilt. In 1908, four members of the Emerson family were killed by lightning while fishing on Bearskull Lake.

Just a coincidence or a result of the curse? Want to find out for yourself? Call 715-561-2922.

Land of the Lumberjacks

All aboard an authentic steam-engine train to ride the rails leading to the Camp Five Museum in Laona. You'll reach the original site of the Connor Lumber and Land Company's 1902 Logging Camp #5, which offers all kinds of lumberjack artifacts and audio-slide shows depicting original logging operations. Call 800-774-3414.

Eau Claire's Paul Bunyan Logging Camp visually entices visitors with displays that explain that rough-and-tumble lifestyle of early Wisconsin loggers, including a bunkhouse, cook's shanty, horse and ox barn, and logging equipment. Call 800-344-3866.

The Menominee Logging Museum in Keshena may be the largest preserved logging camp in the United States. Located on the Wolf River at Grignon Rapids, just below Keshena Falls, the museum includes seven original log buildings and more than 20,000 logging-era artifacts. Call 715-799-3757.

Wisconsin Originals

Concrete Park

Here's a park that celebrates hardcore art—everything's made of concrete. Wisconsin Concrete Park in Phillips is the brainchild of Fred Smith, who at age 65 began sculpting statues of historical and mythical figures.

The self-taught artist, who during his lifetime was a logger, farmer, tavern owner, and musician, conjured up more than 200 figures in all—everyone from Paul Bunyan and his blue ox, Babe, to Abe Lincoln, Sacagawea, and the Statue of Liberty.

Today, the art-filled park is a full-fledged preservation project of the Kohler Foundation, Inc., which supports many artistic endeavors. Call 800-269-4505 or 715-339-4505.

Really Big Fish Story

You've heard of the big one that got away? Well, this one didn't—it's a three-story-high muskie, featuring a balcony that you can step out onto (it's actually the fighting game fish's open mouth).

Sounds loopy? Not at the National Fresh Water Fishing Hall of Fame in Hayward. It claims to be the world's largest fishing museum and features hundreds of mounted trophy fish, more than 800 historic fishing reels, 350 outboards (some not much bigger than your Cuisinart), and even 6,000 lures.

There's a video-fishing theater where anglers can watch tall fishing tales unreel before their eyes. But I like to wander the grounds, where you can take a photograph of yourself landing a really big trophy fish—approximately the size of an elephant. Call 715-634-4440.

Fall

First Capitol Capers

Nope, Madison has not always been the site of Wisconsin's state capitol. The honor goes to Belmont, on County Highway G. In October 1836, this tiny hamlet was the meeting place of 39 very inexperienced state legislators who convened the first legislative session for the old Wisconsin Territory.

They made the most of their short time here, spending much of the cold fall and winter huddling together for 46 days and passing 42 laws. This novice group also established the state judicial system and called for roads and railroads to be built throughout the territory that 12 years later would become the state of Wisconsin.

Oh yes. The legislators also passed one other law—the one establishing Madison as the permanent capitol city.

Today you can visit this picturesque village of Belmont for a firsthand look at the historic First Capitol buildings. Two of the modest frame structures still stand and have been restored to their 1836 appearance. You also can tour the buildings, which feature displays on early territorial Wisconsin and that first legislature. Call 608-987-2122.

For More Information

The state also publishes a 72-page guide loaded with 140 designated Wisconsin-heritage sites, including nine living-history State Historical Society landmarks and more than 50 museums of distinction. You can mine the wealth of this fine guidebook when you receive your own free copy; just call 800-432-8747 and ask for it. Note, however, that the life of state publications depends on demand; the tourism department can decide to stop printing the booklets at any time. So here's hoping that this handsome guidebook is still available!

Wisconsin Originals

36

World-Class Luxury at Canoe Bay

CHETEK

NOT ONLY HAS LUXURIOUS CANOE BAY EARNED THE COVETED Four-Star Award from the *Mobil Travel Guide* making it the only Great Lakes region inn so-honored—but it's also the first and only inn in Wisconsin to receive four stars in the 38-year history of the *Mobil Travel Guide* and one of only 426 elite lodging establishments in North America honored with this distinction.

And now Canoe Bay has become the only Midwest lodging established to be accepted by Relais & Chateaux, the Paris-based association, which includes the finest and most luxurious hotels and lodgings throughout the world.

What an honor for Canoe Bay owners and innkeepers, Dan and Lisa Dobrowolski!

But we also should be thrilled that the innkeepers have put so much of themselves into making Canoe Bay a must-stay destination for the discerning traveler looking for elegance, luxury, and excellence—and I haven't even mentioned the four-star menu of the inn's gourmet restaurant, which overlooks a private lake.

Simply put: You must experience Canoe Bay. And once you do, you'll want to return again and again.

The inn has an interesting history: After six years as a weatherman at WFLD–Channel 32 in Chicago, Dan is now forecasting sunny times at his country inn tucked deep into the forests of northwestern Wisconsin.

"I got up this morning, the sky was bright, and my dad and I caught five bass out on the lake in less than an hour," Dobrowolski said. "How could a day start out any better?"

The affable television personality exchanged the fast track of late-night television news for a 280-acre wilderness tract that includes three private lakes which he wandered with his father more than 30 years ago.

"I spent many memorable summers here," Dobrowolski said. "I never forgot about it, dreamt about it, wondered what it might be like to come back here and relive those kinds of experiences."

He never thought he'd get the chance. Dobrowolski's "piece of heaven" was sold when he was 10. But when this gem recently went up for sale, Dan snatched it back. Lucky for us that he and Lisa decided to share it.

Canoe Bay, a luxurious 16-suite inn, sits on the shore of crystal-clear Lake Wahdoon, a 50-acre spring-fed body of water surrounded by 280 acres of private oak, aspen, and maple forests. It boasts breathtaking views, incomparable service, and complete privacy.

Fashioned in the grand tradition that reflects the influence of Wisconsin native Frank Lloyd Wright, the inn also includes a great room with soaring natural-cedar cathedral ceilings and a 30-foot-tall hand-constructed fieldstone fireplace, considered by its builder to be "the 'Mona Lisa' of fireplaces."

But that's where all comparisons to other woodsy retreats should end. Canoe Bay is a unique combination of North Woods ambience and cosmopolitan flair that resembles showcase homes found in the pages of *Architectural Digest*. In fact, no luxury is spared at this one-of-a-kind sanctuary.

In the great room, behind oversized sofas and chairs surrounding the fireplace, a wall of windows offers one of the most sensational views of lake and woods found at any Midwest hostelry.

The spring-fed lake waters are a sea of calm for guests who want to relax in total tranquility or who are willing to paddle a canoe or rowboat onto the glasslike surfaces. Boaters inevitably see wildlife, including ducks, heron, mink, beaver, and deer.

"Lisa's got something going with a big loon that meets her canoe out in the middle of the lake each morning," Dobrowolski jokes. Also look for an enthusiastic otter that occasionally greets visitors with a splashy hello.

Guest suites offer North Woods–meets–Metropolitan Museum of Art decor, along with two-person whirlpools ("not just glorified bathtubs," Dan emphasizes). The Oak Park Suite boasts a Wright-inspired, 14-foot wall of casement windows overlooking a lake; the Wood Grove Suite allows guests to observe natural surroundings from their platform two-person Jacuzzi through wraparound windows. Also count on the river-rock fireplace, stereo TV/VCR/CD, wet bar with fridge, microwave oven, private deck, and more.

Mornings bring even more pampering, with breakfast baskets delivered to your room or brought out to the patio overlooking the lake where you can enjoy scores of chirping songbirds with your food. Meals might include fresh grapefruit and juices; freshly baked cranberry bread, croissants, and homemade preserves; delicious egg soufflé and cheese plate; and beverages.

You can work off the chow by wandering Canoe Bay's miles of nature trails, which double as cross-country ski paths in winter. One trail leads to a bridge connecting one of the lodge's two islands to the mainland.

Head down to see Snort, a 12-year-old buck that's fenced off in a large preserve, part of Dan's brother-in-law's licensed wild-game breeding farm. "He's just an oversized dog with

World-Class Luxury at Canoe Bay

antlers," Dan said, acknowledging that Snort especially likes being rubbed behind the ears.

Hearty trekkers can head west from the lodge to what Dobrowolski calls his own "Jurassic Park"—bogs, sloughs, blackberry and strawberry patches, and all kinds of natural surprises that haven't been touched for hundreds of years.

Canoe Bay's dining room also offers dinners to guests. Cuisine is extraordinary, featuring deliciously creative gourmet dishes as well as a northern Wisconsin touch, boasting range-fed turkey with locally grown cranberries, Indian-harvested wild rice, fresh-baked breads, fruit pies, and more. And its wine list is one of the most extensive in the midwest.

Canoe Bay's standout season could be autumn, when former weatherman Dobrowolski annually forecasts great colors, noting that leaves from the lodge's oak, aspen, and maple trees span the entire color spectrum—from burnt orange and bright yellow to fiery red. But holidays receive special treatment, too. Between Thanksgiving and New Year's guests get guided cross-country ski tours, ice-skating, ice-fishing, and a 14-foot-tall Christmas tree with all the trimmings. Not to mention a free, personal weather forecast from prognosticator Dan, who is often heard saying, "If there's a better place on earth, I don't know it."

Forget earth. This is heaven.

Fall

For More Information

Canoe Bay rates include a full breakfast; dinners are extra. Chetek is located about 40 miles north of Eau Claire, off U.S. 53. For more information, contact Canoe Bay at P.O. Box 908, W16065 Hogback Road, Chetek, WI 54728, 800-568-1995 or 715-924-4594. Fax 715-924-2078. Website: www.canoebay.com

37

Cave of the Mounds

BLUE MOUNDS

EVER SINCE A QUARRY BLAST ACCIDENTALLY UNCOVERED CAVE of the Mounds in 1939, it has been one of Wisconsin's top tourist attractions. More than 59,000 people poured into the cave, which snakes like a great underground tunnel for about one-third of a mile behind the original quarry wall, in the first 27 weeks after its unearthing. Now, 60 years later, 5 million visitors have walked through its underground chasms.

But it's not a tourist trap or anything close to that. Chicago Academy of Sciences has called the million-year-old cave the most significant in the upper Midwest because of its varied limestone formations. Recently, the U.S. Department of the Interior agreed that the cave is something special and designated it a national natural landmark.

That appellation is likely to add even more bodies to the crush of summer weekend spelunkers who often transform the cave's narrow passageways into a human sardine can. I suggest an early springtime visit to avoid the mobs.

Get there early Sunday morning for the day's first cave tour, which lasts about an hour, and you'll almost have the place to yourself. All tours start with a slide presentation explaining how area limestone develops acidic pockets of mineral-laden water, which eventually dissolve chambers within the rock, leading to more water invasion and the formation of the cave itself.

You'll get a better idea of what all that means once you're inside the cave. It's cool and damp, with temperatures at 50 degrees year-round; you'll also hear the repeated staccato splash of water dripping from the cave's lifeline, major cracks and crevices in the ceiling.

That water continues to create the eerie, otherworldly formations of stalagmites and stalactites, icicles of stone which rise from the cave floor and hang from the ceiling like spooky fingers, and ice-smooth sheets of flowstone that resemble polished onyx. Geologists say it takes from 50 to 150 years for these formations to grow one cubic inch.

It is surprising to discover gleaming columns of colored stone that shimmer like precious gems when the guide's searchlight pierces the darkness. Orange, red, purple, blue, and white blend together in festive bands of rock ribbon along cave walls that call to mind dashing strokes in an artist's painting.

In the "Meanders," a winding stretch of cave passageways lined with cave onyx, you'll reach the lowest point in the cave: 70 feet below the surface. Here you'll also see calcite oysters, tiny flecks in the stone that sparkle like gold.

Another highlight is the "Painted Waterfall," with its brilliant colors caused by oxidized minerals, and the "Reflecting Pool," which once filled the room to the ceiling and today would reach a level of four feet deep if it wasn't periodically drained.

Just off the cave's "Cathedral," a large dome-shaped room, is the "Chapel." Here a series of stone columns closely resemble an old-fashioned pipe organ. I thought it was a rather dreary spot compared to other sections of the cave;

however, several couples have been so enthralled with it that they have been married here.

My favorite part of the cavern is the "Narrows," more crudely referred to as "Fat Man's Misery," or in my case, "Tall Man's Headache." Any predisposition toward claustrophobia will be revealed here. The cave ceiling crops low, and the narrow path twists and turns while it puts the squeeze on all but the most in-shape cave explorers—even sometimes forcing visitors to shuffle sideways through the jagged gaps.

Finally a series of small rooms, or windows, discovered in the 1940s reveal some of the cave's most striking formations: a large stone totem, gleaming "gems," and a "diamond" stalactite that glimmers red when the light is dimmed. Add to that the "Dream River Room," a rock chamber that meanders more than 250 feet into the depths of the cave, revealing marvelous examples of even more delicate formations, and you have an hour's worth of surprises that you won't soon forget.

FOR MORE INFORMATION

Cave of the Mounds is open daily March 15 to November 15, and on weekends only (Saturday and Sunday) during the rest of the year. Admission fees include children's and seniors' rates. It is located four miles west of Mount Horeb, 20 miles west of Madison, just off U.S. 18–151. For more information, contact Cave of the Mounds, Brigham Farm, Blue Mounds, WI 53517, 608-437-3038.

Cave of the Mounds

38

Great River Road

ALONG THE MISSISSIPPI IN WESTERN WISCONSIN

YOU CAN SPEND A DAY, A WEEKEND, OR A MONTH OF SUNdays exploring Wisconsin's portion of the Great River Road (GRR). From Dickeyville in the southwestern corner of the state to St. Croix Falls in the north, this scenic drive flanks the upper Mississippi River for more than 300 miles. Cities and blufftop towns follow the graceful curves of the river, which seemingly offers surprises around every bend.

I especially like to drive the GRR during autumn, when nature's palette brushes the bluffs with a sheen of gold. Apple country is nearby, with scores of orchards offering juicy treats, and Indian caverns and caves bring to mind tales of Huck Finn.

Here are some of this route's most interesting highlights:

In the extreme southwest corner of the state is Dickeyville, home to the Dickeyville Grotto, a religious folk-art shrine built out of stone, seashells, and pieces of colored glass by Fr. Mathias Wernerus. It's open year-round.

In Potosi, you can cruise the town's only road, but this Main Street is more than three miles long.

Cassville boasts the Eagle Nature Preserve, whose midwinter bald eagle population numbers more than 1,000, and a turn-of-the-century living-history museum.

Nearby Gays Mills is the heart of southwestern Wisconsin's apple country. A half-dozen apple farms are ripe for autumn pickings. Springtime visitors will see thousands of fragrant apple blossom trees.

Also close by is Soldiers Grove, destroyed by a 1978 flood and rebuilt as an "all solar city." Visit Solar Town Center to learn more about the sun's energy-producing powers.

If you stopped in Potosi, you can't miss Ferryville, home to the longest street in the world—and one of the narrowest, barely leaving room for State 35 and a railroad wedged between the Mississippi on one side and some high bluffs on the other.

Coon Valley boasts Norskedalen, a 350-acre living-history preserve offering tours by costumed guides through Norwegian pioneer settlements, including log cabins, farm buildings, and craft shops.

La Crosse, the state's largest city on the Mississippi, offers such diversions as rides on the paddle wheeler *La Crosse Queen*; Riverside USA, which explains life on the river; G. Heilmann Brewery tours; and Granddad Bluff, with 1,200-foot vistas of the Mississippi.

Midway's Circle D Buffalo Ranch is home to one of the country's most successful commercial herds with 350 animals.

The entire 1890s Main Street of Trempealeau, named after a river navigation landmark used by French trappers, is listed on the National Register of Historic Places. You also can rent houseboats for Mississippi River adventures. Perrot State Park offers 500-foot river-bluff panoramas, and the city's namesake National Wildlife Refuge is wintering grounds to hundreds of American bald eagles.

Alma, yet another quaint river town, claims only two streets, but they stretch for more than seven miles.

Pepin is the birthplace of Laura Ingalls Wilder, author of the renowned *Little House* children's books, upon which the

Fall

Little House on the Prairie television series was based. It offers a replica of Wilder's birthplace cabin and celebrates Laura Ingalls Wilder Days annually each September; included is a Laura look-alike contest and other "Little House" fun.

Prescott is the state's oldest Mississippi River town, dating back to 1839. Take a self-guided walking tour of historic sites, and head to vistas in Mercord State Park to see where the blue waters of the St. Croix River mix with the muddy brown Mississippi.

Continue along the St. Croix National Scenic Riverway to Hudson, which contains startling examples of elegant turn-of-the-century architecture.

Somerset is the self-proclaimed "tubing capital of the world," offering inner tube rentals for splashy adventures on the Apple River.

The south end of Osceola's business district includes a waterfall.

Finally, St. Croix Falls' Interstate Park offers breathtaking vistas of the Dalles, a steep, narrow gorge cut through rock walls by the St. Croix River. Also visit its Ice Age Interpretive Center to learn about the great glacier that rumbled through Wisconsin more than 10,000 years ago. Or rent canoes and paddle down the designated National Scenic Riverway.

For More Information

For more information about attractions along the Great River Road, contact Wisconsin Division of Tourism, P.O. Box 7606, Madison, WI 53707, 800-432-TRIP (national) or 800-372-2737 (Wisconsin and neighboring states).

Great River Road

.

39

Talking Houses

FOND DU LAC

MR. ED PROVED THAT A HORSE CAN TALK. "MY MOTHER THE Car" did the same for automobiles. But nobody has ever mentioned a talking house—until now.

At least a dozen buildings chatter their roofs off in Fond du Lac, a city nestled against Lake Winnebago in eastern Wisconsin. A combination of historic sites, handsome mansions, and architectural wonders, these "talking houses" are billed as "the first of their kind anywhere in the country." Well, I've heard of whispering oaks and howling winds, but. . . .

This imaginative electronic wrinkle allows visitors sunrise-to-sunset, historic-house touring—without ever having to leave their cars. Just park not more than 200 feet from the front entrance of a building that displays a "talking house" symbol. Each talking house has a radio transmitter operating at 1020 AM on the radio dial. Tune in your car radio (hikers and bikers can adjust their Walkmans), sit back, and listen.

You will hear a taped one- to two-minute message about the building, providing details (complete with sound effects) on its year of construction, original owners, historic uses, and other facts. When the broadcast is completed, just move on to the next site.

Talking-house tour maps are available at Fond du Lac motels, restaurants, and the visitors bureau. It should take about two hours to complete the circuit of homes.

The self-guided tour includes many of the town's most architecturally interesting structures. One of the finest is an 1882 Queen Anne home built with twin-turreted Norman towers. Located at 199 East Division Street, the house features four vibrant exterior colors (most recently cranberry pink, ballad pink, rendezvous purple, and green), extensive woodworking inside, and a second-floor ballroom.

At St. Paul's Cathedral, 51 West Division Street, you will learn that the church's unusual wood carvings, done in Oberammergau, Germany, are considered some of the finest in the United States. The stone cathedral also has impressive stained-glass windows.

Pull up to the Octagon House, 276 Linden Street, and you'll see a stop on the slave-saving Underground Railroad. Built in 1856 by Isaac Brown as a fortress, the home offers tours (Monday through Saturday) of its nine passageways and an underground tunnel, plus candlelight tours during July and December.

Drive out to Old Pioneer Road (southeast of the city limits) to see Galloway House and Village. The 30-room, white-clapboard mansion with red-shingled roof was built in 1868 and is open for tours from Memorial Day through Labor Day. It is surrounded by 23 historic structures, including a photographer's shop, store, and church, all depicting life at the turn of the century.

Another dazzler is a Greek Revival mansion, long considered one of Fond du Lac's choicest architectural plums. Built in 1927, the 11-room building at 245 East Divi-

Fall

sion Street is graced by four massive porch columns reminiscent of Virginia plantation homes.

For More Information

For more talking house and area information, contact Fond du Lac Convention and Visitors Bureau, 19 West Scott Street, Fond du Lac, WI 54935, 800-937-9123 or 920-923-3010.

Talking Houses

40

Holy Hill

HUBERTUS

IN 1855 A MAN IN A TOWN CALLED ERIN LABORED FOR WEEKS to build a massive wooden cross and place it atop one of the highest hills in the Kettle Moraine region. It could be seen for miles around, a stark sentinel standing strangely in the jumble of hills, holes, and ridges carved out by the last great glacier more than 10,000 years ago.

The cross quickly became an object of curiosity. But it wasn't until a French hermit worshipped at the foot of the cross and experienced a "miraculous cure" that waves of pilgrims flocked to Holy Hill in Hubertus in great numbers.

Today, Holy Hill continues to draw thousands of visitors to its spectacular setting of natural beauty. However, a large church now perches precariously atop the hillside, listing like the leaning tower of Pisa. Like its more simple predecessor, its spires are visible from miles away, reaching high into the heavens.

The house of prayer, listed on the National Register of Historic Places and designated as a "National Shrine of Mary, Help of Christians," is itself inspiring, built in neo-Romanesque design with priceless stained-glass windows and magnificent mosaics.

Yet it's inside the Shrine Chapel located off the main body of the church, that people find the most inspiration. Here you'll see crutches, canes, and other worldy mementos lining the walls of the chapel that houses a statue of Mary presenting her son, Jesus, to all believers. Many continue to seek her help and intercession for their problems and troubles.

During summer and fall thousands of visitors also climb 178 steps to the apex of the church's observation tower located inside one of its tall spires. They're rewarded with breathtaking views of the glacially carved landscape, as well as the skyline of Milwaukee, about 30 miles south on the horizon.

The shrine is a perfect place for peaceful relaxation and meditation. Staffed by the Discalced Carmelite Friars and others, there is a full weekend Mass schedule (everyone is invited), along with Marian devotions, daily religious services, and other Roman Catholic sacraments for those who desire them.

Go for a walk along a half-mile outdoor trail dotted with 14 groups of life-size sculptures depicting the Way of the Cross (representing the Passion of Jesus). Or visit the "Lourdes Grotto," a replica of the French cave where Mary is said to have appeared to a group of peasant children around the turn of the century. You may want to simply stroll the shrine's 400 acres, part of which are crossed by Wisconsin's Ice Age Trail, one of the country's premier trekking paths.

For overnight stays at the shrine, simple guest rooms are available with advance reservations. The Old Monastery Inn offers meals, snacks, and Sunday brunch. Special seasonal events occur throughout the year; highlights include a living Nativity at Christmas, religious concerts, and a summer arts-and-crafts fair.

For More Information

Holy Hill is open year-round; admission and parking are free. It is located five miles south of Hartford, on State 167. For more information contact Holy Hill, 1525 Carmel Road, Hubertus, WI 53033, 414-628-1838.

Holy Hill

41

Hiking the Ice Age Trail

IT'S A 1,000-MILE JOURNEY PAST GLACIAL GHOSTS WINDING across forests, parks, and private lands. Stretching from the Door County Peninsula in the east and looping up and down until reaching the St. Croix River in the west, a magical landscape unfolds that is part majesty and part millennia.

And the best way to explore it is by walking.

Wisconsin's Ice Age Trail, which follows the path carved by the last great glacier more than 10,000 years ago, is one of the most exciting trekking adventures in the Midwest. Edging the terminal moraine (rock, boulders, and stone-laden soil) of the primordial ice sheet that melted in a rush of rotting ice and flooding water even before man took a step on the planet, the trail is a wonderland of glacial thrills.

It's been called the "country's best glacier signature," with geologic features that include giant bowl-shaped depressions, snakelike ridges, long rounded hills, and old glacial lakes. Today 475 miles of this designated National Scenic Trail are open to hikers; another 525 miles will eventually be added so that the Ice Age Trail rivals other great national paths like the Lewis and Clark Trail and the Natchez Trace.

Take an hour or a day to explore the trail, divided into segments and posted with familiar triangular markers.

Mountain bikers can pedal across geologic history. In winter it's open to cross-country skiing.

To get a dose of history, along with fabulous glacially carved vistas, you might start at the Ice Age Interpretive Center, in Interstate Park, just south of St. Croix. The center features exhibits explaining Wisconsin's glacier period; it also offers a 20-minute film, *Night of the Sun*, which details how the glacier maintained its icy grip on the landscape.

Summer interpretive programs include ranger-led trail hikes. Highlights include the Dalles of the St. Croix River—narrow, steep-sided gorges carved by the rushing meltwaters of the glacier; and a series of "potholes" literally drilled into the rock by glacial fury, for which the park is famous.

Another portion of the trail stretches 40 miles through the Chequamegon National Forest in northwestern Wisconsin (northwest of Medford). While tall spruce and hemlock trees of these North Woods seem to touch the heavens, you'll see old gray stumps of huge virgin pines clear-cut by timbermen more than 100 years ago. Their charred remains point to the ongoing conflict between progress (these forests built great cities like Chicago) and the preservation of the natural world.

The most lofty vistas are contained in the Sauk County trail segment that winds through Devil's Lake State Park offering sweeping panoramas of both the Baraboo Valley and ancient glacial lakes. Resistant rock of the Baraboo Bluffs stopped the glacier's advance in these parts; as a result the glacier gouged and plucked—and then quit.

What all this means is that hikers scale 500-foot bluffs yielding breathtaking panoramas of glacial topography. If you're one of them, you'll see everything from boulder-strewn shorelines and rocky bluff outcroppings to "extinct" glacial lakes. It's also great topography for rock climbing, and several schools offer weekend-long lessons that teach you how to scale these craggy peaks.

My favorite part of the trail remains Kettle Moraine State Forest—the northern unit is located between Plymouth and Campbellsport on State 67 (see Chapter 32). Part of the Ice Age National Scientific Reserve, the forest offers ranger-led hikes, talks, and guided tours in summer to some of the most well-known glacial features seen here—including Dundee Mountain (glacial debris); Parnell Esker (a long, snakelike ridge); and Greenbush Kettle (a huge bowl-shaped depression).

First-time hikers should stop inside the Henry S. Reuss Ice Age Visitor Center (located a half-mile south of Dundee, on State 57) for an introduction to the local glacial landscape. Exhibits and films depict glacial history of the region and explain what it is you will see along the trail.

What I haven't yet mentioned are all the other natural wonders along the trail: wild plums and bittersweet blossoms in summer; beavers who dam up glacial bogs and build huge lodges; massive gray boulders, each weighing tons, stacked in piles hundreds of yards high, seemingly teetering in prelude to an avalanche and covered with bright green moss and lichens; deer spiriting their young along curvy eskers; hawks circling over meadows like patrolling fighter pilots.

The last word of advice: Take your time. Nature did.

FOR MORE INFORMATION

For more Ice Age Trail hiking information, contact Ice Age Trail, Wisconsin Department of Natural Resources, P.O. Box 7921, Madison, WI 53707, 608-266-2181; Ice Age, North Country and Lewis and Clark National Trails Office, Suite 100, 700 Rayovac Drive, Madison, WI 53711, 608-264-5610; Ice Age Interpretive Center, P.O. Box 703, St. Croix Falls, WI 54024, 715-483-3747; Henry S. Reuss Ice Age Visitor Center, P.O. Box 410, Campbellsport, WI 53010, 414-594-6200.

Hiking the Ice Age Trail

Winter

42

Winter Magic

WINTER IS MAGICAL IN WISCONSIN. FROZEN LANDSCAPES sculpted into mythical shapes create a fantasyland of ice and snow. Outdoor fun centers on edge-of-your-seat thrills: downhill powder skiing; North Woods cross-country touring; making tracks on snowshoes across snow-blanketed ice-age trails; and roaring by snowmobile along the shores of the Great Lakes, past ice caves and blue ice shelves.

It's also one of the best times to take advantage of charming lodges, inns, and boutique hotels. The five described here place you right on the doorstep of cold-season adventures.

On a clear night, the northern lights shimmer in the sky above the Old Rittenhouse Inn, in Bayfield, a historic fishing village on Lake Superior's south shore. Inside, innkeeper Jerry Phillips, resplendent in a black velvet Victorian vest, renders a mouth-watering summary of the evening's dinner choices: they might include steak Bercy (stuffed with oysters), Lake Superior trout *aux champagne*, pork ragout, and fruit-glazed chicken cordon bleu. His wife, Mary, cooks as many as 75 five-course meals a night, while Jerry creates such desserts as white-chocolate cheesecake.

"I love cooking for guests," says Mary, "and I won't change till the day I die."

Pampering is their specialty at the three-story, 18-room

Queen Anne mansion (a town landmark since 1890), with its gabled roof and huge wraparound veranda. Gracious guest rooms feature fine Victorian antiques. Some have fireplaces, adding flickering flames of romance to winter evenings that sometimes howl with subzero wind chills; others offer window views of blustery Lake Superior.

"Bayfield is a quiet little village in winter," Mary remarks. "People love to experience the solitude of a winter outing, then come back to the excitement of all the people at the inn."

Jerry believes in a civilized breakfast to prepare guests for cold-weather wanderings. Soothing chamber music wafts through the Victorian dining room, with a morning fire blazing in the hearth. Initial courses like brandied peaches and blueberries in cream are followed by New Orleans–style cinnamon French toast or red raspberry crepes.

Just down the street is headquarters for Trek & Trail, an adventure outfitter that offers all kinds of winter fun. That includes guided tours of Squaw Bay sea caves, some cutting more than 60 feet into high cliffs, creating magnificent ice arches. Try cross-country ski trips to the Apostle Islands National Lakeshore. Other do-it-yourself cold-weather fun includes downhill thrills at nearby Mount Ashwabay and Mount Valhalla, in the Chequamegon National Forest.

"It is a romantic setting," Mary says of Bayfield's rugged winter landscape, "picturesque like the vast Russian forests in *Doctor Zhivago*—only not as cold as Siberia." The inn is open all year; weekends only, November through April. Contact the inn at 301 Rittenhouse Avenue, Bayfield, WI 54814, 715-779-5765; for Trek & Trail information, call 715-779-3320.

Who would expect to find an authentic Irish guest house in the middle of the Dairy State? Cary ("Rip") O'Dwanny, a robust Irishman with tufts of red hair and the wry smile of a leprechaun, has fashioned a little bit o' "auld sod" at 52

Stafford, in Plymouth. On winter weekends Irish jigs and reels echo through the inn's pub with its imposing cherrywood bar. Guests warm themselves by the saloon fireplace. Guinness Stout and Harp Lager flow from the tap, along with good times.

"I wanted a place where guests could feel at home in a tuxedo or blue jeans," O'Dwanny said. A visiting singer from Belfast once passed through the inn's arched doorway, looked around with a smile, and proclaimed in a thick brogue, "Ah, just like home."

O'Dwanny has used the finest European materials to decorate the inn. There are tables topped with Carrara marble, handmade English carpeting, and exquisite leaded glass from West Germany. Wingback chairs are upholstered in Chinese silk. The woodwork on the first floor is solid cherry, and there are brass chandeliers to lend a classical air. Guest rooms have bright English, floral wallpapers and four-poster beds. The building, constructed in 1892, is listed on the National Register of Historic Places.

An avid skier and former president of a local ski club, O'Dwanny takes his winter fun seriously. Many of his guests do, too, especially when they discover that Greenbush, one of the state's top-rated cross-country ski areas, with 30 miles of groomed trails, is only five miles west of the inn. Fishermen will be pleased to learn that local trout streams can be fished even in winter because churning stream channels prevent freezing in all but the coldest weather. And it's only a 30-minute drive to Lake Winnebago, which does freeze every winter to become the home of 4,000 ice-fishing shanties—painted in every hue, often with stripes or polka dots for added effect.

This colorful shantytown, dubbed "Sturgeon City" by locals, is a spectacle not to be missed. If you get a sudden urge to try your luck at hooking a walleye or spearing a sturgeon, local outfitters rent all the equipment, including a shanty. A bottle of "cottontail" (brandy mixed with peppermint schnapps), a local ice fisherman favorite, is optional.

Says O'Dwanny, "When guests come in from the cold with their noses runny and red, I fix them an Irish coffee or an Irish whiskey, and soon they're feeling very special."

Open all year, there are 20 rooms, all with private baths. Contact the inn at 52 Stafford Street, Plymouth, WI 53703, 920-893-0552.

The central Wisconsin town of Green Lake is the oldest resort community west of Niagara Falls. The Heidel House Resort, hugging the wooded shoreline of the deep, seven-mile-long lake, is an elegant four-seasons hotel offering breathtaking lakeside views and lots of winter fun.

Many people from surrounding big cities who just want to escape after the holiday craziness come here. Their goal is relaxation in the midst of a winter wonderland.

The 200-room hotel boasts everything from main-lodge guest rooms with deluxe lake views, to Lac Verde Lodge suites with private balconies, to cottages dotting the grounds. You can gaze out over the lake, where you're likely to see cross-country skiers skimming the shoreline and ice-boats with colorful sails gliding across the frozen waters.

Romantic lakeside dining is the treat at the hotel's Grey Rock Mansion featuring gourmet-style food. Or head to the Boathouse Lounge and Eatery for live entertainment.

Green Lake is a hotbed for iceboat racing. The sleek craft resemble bobsleds but have huge triangular mainsails that unfurl to catch the wind, plus three bottom runners, or blades. They glide over frozen lakes at breakneck speeds.

Those piloting the one-person boats must simultaneously shift body weight, steer, and adjust the sail to achieve maximum speeds. Yet, they're only a few inches off the ice and going 75 mph.

Winter

Top Midwestern ice pilots often compete during official January boat races on Green Lake. It also has been the site of sanctioned international yacht racing featuring world-class racers from the United States, Canada, and Europe.

Cross-country skiing is also a passion here, with miles of groomed trails passing through pine and maple woodlands, along rocky cliffs, and down sloping lakeshore. The 1,100-acre, Baptist-run Green Lake Center has trails passing stone towers and old estate houses with panoramic views of the water. The Heidel House offers ski touring packages; there is a terrific view of the ice-covered lake from its heated indoor pool. And Green Lake sprouts its own "Shantytown" of hearty ice fishermen. Contact the hotel at 643 Illinois Avenue, Green Lake, WI 54941, 920-294-3344.

Westby is located on a ridge between the Mississippi River's Coulee Region and the Kickapoo River Valley, a short drive from La Crosse. Ninety percent of its 2,000 townspeople are of Norwegian descent, according to Patricia Benjamin Smith. "You still hear a lot of it [the Norwegian language] in town," she says. In fact, Westby had its own Norwegian-language newspaper until just after World War II.

Smith owns Westby House, a landmark Victorian mansion with a Queen Anne tower, stained-glass windows, and gingerbread finery. It was built in the 1890s by Martin Bekkedahl, a Norse immigrant who ran a successful tobacco farm here in the mid-1800s and sponsored people from his homeland to work the fields. The inn's four guest rooms are spacious and small-town charming, with brass and iron-rail beds, lacy window curtains, and country quilts. "We want people to feel warm and toasty, to just rest and hole up if they want to."

With its Scandinavian bent, it is not surprising that Westby would become the Midwestern home of ski jumping. The 11 jumps in town are used to train everyone from tots to Olympic hopefuls.

Winter Magic

The big 90-meter hill is the same size as ones used for jumping events in Lake Placid and the Olympic Winter Games, locals say. You can watch skiers soar through the air during the annual Snowflake International 90 Meter Ski Jumping Tournament held in February at nearby Timber Coulee. Members of the U.S. Ski Jumping team, and national teams of Canada, Finland, and Norway often compete in Olympic-style contests here.

Timber Coulee is one of the few jumps where spectators can park cars along the outrun and keep warm while watching ski jumpers land. Loudspeakers announce results of each jump, and a local radio station provides coverage.

While the jumps can be used by everyone, first-timers restrict themselves to a five-meter hill that shoots daredevils about 20 feet into the air. The less adventurous might opt to hit cross-country trails (three within five miles, with lights for night touring) or go downhill at Mount La Crosse, northwest of Westby.

Just watching world-class jumpers soar 300 feet through the air can create a Norwegian-size appetite. A Westby House specialty is *torsk*, Norwegian cod baked in lemon butter and served with egg noodles. Sunday brunches feature homemade *sodtsuppe* (fruit soup in a tapioca base), *limpa* (dark rye bread), *rommegrot* (cream pudding), and *crumkake* (crumb cake). Contact the Westby House at 200 West State Street, Westby, WI, 54667, 608-634-4112.

Tuxedo-clad menservants greet visitors at the Mansion Hill Inn, an architectural showplace in Madison, the state capital. The mansion was built in 1858 of fine white sandstone from Mississippi River cliffs, Carrara marble from Italy, and ornamental cast iron from Sweden. A $2 million restoration has recaptured its elegance.

The atmosphere is very intimate, romantic, and decadent, with 11 opulent guest rooms boasting exquisite antiques and reproductions, many of the rooms with fireplaces and large whirlpools. Even with a full house, people get the feeling that they're the only ones staying at the inn, a great escape from the cold world outside.

Those who choose to wander Madison, situated on an isthmus between Lakes Mendota and Monona, find that it revels in cold-weather fun. A winter carnival, held in late January, features sled-dog races, ice and snow sculptures, and other frigid madness.

Cross-country skiing is just a matter of slipping on your skis and gliding out the door to one of the city's many green-belts. There's also ice-skating, curling, hockey, broomball, snowshoeing, horseback riding, snow tubing, sleigh rides—an almost limitless number of choices.

With five ski resorts a short drive away, there is plenty of downhill action, too. Cascade Mountain's steep North Wall, whose trails zigzag through woodlands, is as close to Colorado skiing as you'll find in the Midwest.

Return to Mansion Hill from a frosty day outdoors and you'll be treated to hot wine and chocolate truffles. Later travel downtown in style in one of the inn's two Rolls-Royce Silver Clouds and get an elegant dinner. Contact the inn at 424 North Pinckney Street, Madison, WI 53707, 608-255-3999.

Winter Magic

43

Cedarburg Christmas

CEDARBURG

When I think of a Midwest country Christmas, it's hard to imagine a more perfect setting than historic Cedarburg.

The once-thriving woolen mill town that supplied material for the uniforms of Union troops during the Civil War boasts more historic 1800s-era cream-city brick buildings than almost any other town west of Philadelphia. In fact, all of Cedarburg is listed on the National Register of Historic Places.

Today this little 1845 village located just north of Milwaukee revels in the same distinctive holiday appearance that it displayed more than 100 years ago: charming stone houses bedecked with seasonal trimmings, artisans busy in project-filled workshops, and strolling carolers filling the winter air with joyous sounds.

While any holiday-season weekend offers travelers a chance to experience this old-fashioned Christmas spirit, the best time to enjoy Cedarburg's gala holiday atmosphere is during "Christmas in the Country," traditionally held Thursday through Sunday during the first weekend of December.

The annual arts and crafts festival and sale boasts a nationally renowned holiday boutique featuring more than

50 of the state's finest artisans. Housed at Cedar Creek Settlement, the name given to the historic mill buildings themselves, the Christmas bazaar offers everything from handcarved wooden Santas, goose-feather Christmas trees, and embroidered folk dolls to wearable art, kids' toys, and homemade treats from the fest's Christmas kitchen.

Craft-fest junkies should also note that at least one-third of all wares are newly created by artisans each year, and their first exhibit is exclusive to the Cedarburg show. Besides the craft show, there are more than 30 specialty shops selling holiday gifts at Cedar Creek Settlement. Check out boxed sets of Christmas wines at Cedar Creek Winery; Marline's Christmas Shop, stuffed with thousands of tree trimmings and decorations; Dime A Dance and its one-of-a-kind, handcrafted Beary Patch Bears; and the smithy at Cedar Creek Forge, who can hammer out on his anvil all kinds of iron gewgaw stocking stuffers.

Later walk the streets of Cedarburg, twinkling with tiny white holiday lights, to discover more seasonal surprises.

The Festival of Trees, at the Cedarburg Cultural Center, usually coincides with the Christmas craft extravaganza. Gawk at a dazzling display of decorated Christmas trees and holiday wreaths conjured up by local craftspeople. There will also be live entertainment, a kids' corner with toys and games, a gingerbread village, and a Santa hotline for kids to call the North Pole and talk to Saint Nick himself.

That Christmas Feeling, at the Cedarburg Community Center also on the first weekend in December, is another holiday craft bazaar featuring more than 40 booths of artisans' works along with a Candy Cane Shoppe stuffed with homebaked treats.

Another favorite is the annual "Visit With Santa" at the Cedarburg Cultural Center, usually held the second and third Saturdays in December. Kids queue up to chat with Mr. and Mrs. Claus; soon they're amazed when the jolly fat one greets them by their first names. (How'd he know that? 'Cause he's Santa.) Finally children pose with Saint Nick and receive a free photo of their holiday visit.

At Washington Avenue and State 57 also take a peek at the 1855 Cedarburg Mill, a five-story downtown building overlooking Cedar Creek. One of the most impressive in the Midwest, at its zenith this mill produced 120 barrels of fine flour daily.

While you're there, take a short drive to the 1876 Cedarburg Covered Bridge, believed to be the last covered bridge in Wisconsin. Built of 3-inch by 10-inch planks secured by hardwood pins, the bridge is located in a pretty park of winter wonderland scenery three miles north of Cedarburg, at Covered Bridge Road (the junction of State 60 and 143).

Even though Cedarburg is in the shadows of Milwaukee and less than a two-hour drive from Chicago, it's fun to prolong your old-fashioned holiday-season weekend by overnighting at one of the village's quaint country inns. The Washington House Inn, an elegant 1886 Victorian hotel, and the Stagecoach Inn, a restored mid-1800s stagecoach stopover, are excellent choices.

Of course, any time is a good time to visit Cedarburg. Shops are open year-round, and the town offers a full calendar of annual festivals. Highlights include the Winter Festival, first weekend in February; A Day in the Country Folk Art Fair, third weekend in April; Strawberry Festival and Folk Art Fair, third weekend in June; Wine and Harvest Festival, third weekend in September; and Christmas in the Country, first week of December.

Cedarburg Christmas

FOR MORE INFORMATION

There are admission charges for Christmas in the Country, Festival of Trees, and That Christmas Feeling. For dates, prices, and hours, contact Cedar Creek Settlement, N70 W6340 Bridge Road, Cedarburg, WI 53012, 414-375-9390 or 800-827-8020; Cedarburg Visitor Information Center, W63 N645 Washington Avenue, P.O. Box 204, Cedarburg, WI 53012, 414-377-9620.

Winter

44

Downhill Thrills

DOWNHILL THRILLS IN WISCONSIN DON'T MEAN BOWL-FILLED, powder-perfect runs so high in the sky that they seem to teeter on the spine of the Continental Divide. But the Dairy State's ski resorts do include a treasure trove of glacial topography that includes steep, narrow bluff-top ridges, adrenalin-pumping headwalls, and tough hillside runs—more than enough to satisfy any dedicated schusser.

In fact, Wisconsin offers nearly 40 downhill sites, more than any other state east of the Mississippi. It doesn't simply rely on mountain microclimates or Calgary clippers to produce snow; high-volume snow equipment "brings" the snow here. Also, you don't have to be an expert to hit the slopes; scores of these resorts cater to beginners and kids.

And what variety. Want a weekend with European flavor? How about moguls the size of Volkswagens? Skiing with the family? Yahoo night skiing? Wisconsin's got them all.

European Atmosphere

It has been said by seasoned skiers that Alpine Valley's ski runs sometimes remind them of mild European mountain-cruising trails (use your imagination, OK?). But its Euro-lodge definitely will have you thinking "Continental." Alpine's 388-foot vertical drop is enough to fuel solid intermediate runs like "Lodge Express" and "Broadway." Most popular is "Big Thunder," a mogul-strewn nightmare from top to bottom. There are plenty of beginner runs, and the resort provides the state's largest system of double and triple chairlifts carrying schussers to the summit.

The 128-room Old World lodge features dining rooms, lounges with live weekend entertainment, an indoor pool with sauna and whirlpool, ski shops, and a video game room. Contact Alpine Valley, Box 615, East Troy, WI 53120, 414-642-7374.

Mogul Monster

Cascade Mountain, located in Portage, earns kudos as the "best day-ski area in the Midwest." The bluff-top resort, with 21 trails and a 460-foot vertical drop, offers beginner skiing, daily night skiing, and plenty of instruction courses for the kids. Challenging runs include "Radical Rob," which is cut into the eastern edge of the mountain; and "Screamin' Steven," another fright-inducing intermediate slope. However, Cascade has built its reputation as a mogul-lover's delight. Just point your skis downhill on the "Mogul Monster" run to see what I mean; the super-steep chute is dotted with frozen snow lumps the size of Volkswagens. Contact Cascade Mountain, Route 2, Box 138A, Portage, WI 53901, 608-742-5588 or 800-992-2754.

Skiing Rockies-Style

Whitecap Mountains Ski Area, in Montreal, offers some of the state's best powder pleasures. Nearly 40 ski runs are carved into three mountains boasting Colorado-like vistas of sprawling virgin pine forests. While most trails cater to intermediate skiers, you do find a couple of expert runs (narrow and steep, with a 400-foot vertical) on the windward side of the mountains. The nearby town of Hurley remains an *après-ski* paradise for late-night carousers, with nearly 30 bars in a community of only 2,000 permanent residents. For information, contact Whitecap Mountains, Montreal, WI 54550, 715-561-2227; for lodging in area condos and hotels, call 715-561-2776.

Beginner's Paradise

Most skiers I know got their start on Wilmot Mountain, in Wilmot, only sixty miles from Chicago. Nearly thirty runs are carved across 120 hilly acres of skiable terrain that includes advanced runs like Snow Bowl, the Sundance mogul master, and short practice trails that are confidence builders for beginners. All ski trails are lighted for night schussing, and there are learn-to-ski packages that have taught thousands of Chicagoans how to perfect their downhill technique. Contact Wilmot Mountain, Highway W, Wilmot, WI 53192, 414-862-2301.

Family Skiing

Because of its relatively small size, Tyrol Basin in Mount Horeb can be a family paradise of sorts. Its 11 runs include beginner slopes and a long intermediate trail ("Sunrise") that winds through picturesque woods. The family that skis well and together might challenge the "Bump Buster," perhaps Tyrol's most difficult run, a short but nearly vertical head-wall that could even take the breath away from "out-West" ski veterans. For information contact Tyrol Basin Ski Area, 3487 Bohn Road, Mount Horeb, WI 53572, 608-437-4135.

Free Ski

First-time skiers can discover the joys of downhill during annual "Learn to Ski—Free" days on special dates, usually in December or January. Beginners get a free area lift ticket, rental equipment, and a beginner group lesson at participating ski areas across the state. It's a good idea to call ahead for reservations at the ski area of your choice. For "ski free" information, call 800-372-2737.

FOR MORE INFORMATION

Several Wisconsin ski areas do not have overnight lodging. For accommodations or a list of statewide hotels and motels, contact the ski area of your choice or Wisconsin Innkeepers Association, 509 West Wisconsin Avenue, Suite 622, Milwaukee, WI 53203, 414-782-2851. For snow conditions, call the Wisconsin winter snow hotline, operated December through March by the state's tourism department, at 608-266-9575.

45

Ice Fishing Follies

PACK AWAY THE FLIES AND CREELS. BREAK OUT THE "SNOW-mo" suits, buckets, ice augers, and jig poles. And don't forget a bottle of cottontail to keep things toasty. It's time for more great ice-fishing adventures.

Wisconsin boasts plenty of thrills for winter anglers, with nearly 15,000 inland lakes totaling almost one million acres; 235 miles of Mississippi River and its backwaters; and the deep, frozen inlets of Green Bay. Cut a hole in the ice and you could pull out anything from tough fighters like walleye and northern pike to perch and bluegills.

There's even more excitement during the late winter, when Wisconsin's 14-day sturgeon-spearing season opens on Lake Winnebago, the state's largest inland lake. Some of those ugly monsters can weigh more than 100 pounds. Keep in mind that sturgeon caviar is an international delicacy, while smoked sturgeon steaks are a more down-to-earth treat.

Here's what happened on my last winter excursion to Lake Winnebago. I like to call it "Ice Fishing Follies at Sturgeon City."

Cold sleek rain slanted down from a dark-gray sky, trailed by icy winds. Seven people were crammed into a tiny wooden shanty, warmed only by a battered space heater—

and a bottle of cottontail, that delectable concoction of brandy and peppermint schnapps.

A little guy from Verona had me in a vicelike grip, toasting the wonders of sturgeon, perhaps the ugliest fish ever to swim God's waters. Had I fallen into Dante's rings of hell? Nah, I was only ice fishing.

I had been taken hostage by some Wisconsin friends who drove a snowplow, four-by-four, and station wagon over the somewhat frozen surface of Lake Winnebago just so we could stare through holes poked in the ice and angle for walleye. Begging for my release, I knew it was time for desperate measures.

I promised to eat cheese curds and wash 'em down with Cherry wine, attend the next *lutefisk* dinner festival, pretend the Brewers were still a major league–caliber baseball team.

Nothing worked. We cruised over the slushy lake, its surface punctuated by seams and cracks (maybe it just looked that way to this cranky ice fisherman) and deep puddles of water on our way to shanties nearly three miles from shore. We passed "Shantytown" or "Sturgeon City," the lake's "City Without a ZIP Code," where scores of shanties hugged the ice.

Most are small rectangular boxes, some painted wild hues of purple, red, or yellow. Many are sparsely furnished with an old heater and discarded kitchen chairs. But some have paneling, a makeshift kitchenette, comfy padded chairs, television, stereo, CD player, and bar.

Our guide, a local from a "bar and harbor" outfitter in Fond du Lac, said more than 4,000 shanties spring up during sturgeon season. He busily augered holes in the two-foot-thick ice near our shanty. He placed tip-ups (something like automatic fishermen that allow human fishermen to stay somewhat warm in shanties) baited with minnows to attract walleye.

It was not a fun day for him. Besides setting up rigs in a driving rain, he was troubled about fishing conditions.

"We're getting lots of action, but the fish are small," he said. "We had too much cold weather too soon in December. Drove all the big ones down."

"Uh-huh," I said sympathetically.

"Now sturgeon season is here, and there might not even be ice if the rain keeps up," he said. "And we wait all year for that, because it's the ultimate."

"Oh yeah," I agreed in a manly Hemingway manner while dreaming about being bundled up in my grandmother's quilt watching pro golfers in steamy Florida trying to avoid sand traps and rogue alligators.

But you see, sturgeon spearing is serious machismo. You cut a hole six feet across in the ice and try to attract the huge, curious fish with large objects—anything from toilet seats to vacuum cleaners, I'm told. Then you stare at the hole waiting patiently to thrust a seven-foot-long spear through a hideous-looking fish weighing as much as 145 pounds.

At this point, I was inside the shanty jiggling four little minnow-baited poles through holes punched in the ice floor. Amid all the drinking, someone noticed the red flag flying on a tip-up. I was elected to wade into the rain and slush and make the catch. It was a 12-inch walleye, weighing maybe a half pound. Not quite suitable for mounting, I presume.

My friends were unimpressed, too, but we still managed a few toasts. Then we climbed into our rides, non-imbibing designated drivers at the wheel, and headed to shore.

It was thrilling. We got stuck in a deep puddle that threatened to open into a giant fissure and swallow us whole. Then our brakes were so wet we couldn't stop; when the snowplow ahead of us suddenly halted to chat with a pass-

Ice Fishing Follies

ing pickup, we hit the brakes and simply kept going, swerving off the lake's ice road and into even deeper slush and snow, narrowly missing the plow's hind end.

But by now we didn't care. We were ice fishermen. And we recited our oath:

> *Our dream's to spear a sturgeon*
> *We're manly men, we're tough*
> *We'll gaff'em through till they're stiff as glue*
> *And drink and sweat and stuff.*

FOR MORE INFORMATION

For more Wisconsin winter fishing information, contact the University of Wisconsin Sea Grant Institute, Communications Office, 1800 University Avenue, Madison, WI 53705, 608-263-3259; it offers a 20-page illustrated booklet noting fishing regulations, clothing, equipment, and techniques. For books and maps detailing ice-fishing areas in more than 1,000 Wisconsin lakes, contact Fishing Hot Spots, Inc., P.O. Box 1167, Rhinelander, WI 54501, 800-338-5957; for a free booklet on Wisconsin Fishing Guides, contact Wisconsin Tourism Development, P.O. Box 7606, Madison, WI 53707, 608-266-2161 or 800-372-2737.

46

Snow Train

NORTH FREEDOM

"ALL ABOARD," SHOUTS THE CONDUCTOR AS HE HOPS ABOARD the train. Then a shrill whistle shatters the silence, echoing across the hills. Next the great engine roars to life, belching dark clouds of steam into the Wisconsin winter sky.

As the 10-wheel locomotive shudders to life, it slowly begins its one-hour chug through the snow-covered woods, scenic river valleys, and ancient mountain ranges of Sauk County, near Baraboo.

Its load includes several steam-heated antique passenger cars that allow train lovers to relive the golden age of railroading. Camera buffs at trackside can capture scenes of a bygone era as plumes of smoke rise above the treetops and snow-laden valleys.

The nostalgia is all part of the annual Steam Snow Train, the showcase winter spectacle of the Mid-Continent Railway Museum, held in North Freedom the third full weekend of February.

The fun begins Friday morning when a special snowplow engine rolls down the tracks from the museum's vintage 1894 depot. Built in 1906, the huge wooden-wedge plow nudges massive mounds of snow from the rails so later steam trains can roll. At least everybody hopes there will be lots of snow.

Photographers should be ready for three designated excursions during the day to ride special snow trains that include photo run-bys. A night photo session offers opportunities to set up tripods both in the depot area and along the tracks throughout the countryside.

The newest thrill in the Snow Train schedule is a romantic ride on a dinner train, which runs both Friday and Saturday evenings. Tickets are required and reservations are necessary.

Regular snow-train passenger trips begin their nine-mile, roundtrip chugs from the depot, past the mining ghost town of La Rue, and up to Quartzite Lake on Saturday and Sunday, running six times daily. Venerable steam engines that have made past runs include the *Saginaw Timber No. 2*, built in 1912 for shortline lumber hauls in Michigan; the *Western Coal & Coke No. 1*, built in 1913 in Canada; and the *Chicago and North Western No. 1385*, built in 1907.

Steam-heated cars include first-class service in a Pullmanlike carriage; there is an extra admission charge for this service, which includes snacks and drinks served by white-coated waitstaff. Or you can sit in an antique coach car for the price of a regular ticket.

Weather permitting, there often are special steam-engine freight runs both weekend days, following three of the passenger trains. The fun here is centered on seating in an antique caboose, outfitted with an operating coal stove to keep things toasty.

In addition to the rail runs, films and demonstrations in the Freight House explain Operation Lifesaver, a rail-crossing safety program aimed especially at kids. Tours of the Coach Shed feature restored cars and other rail equipment, and a period depot—complete with operating telegraph, potbelly stove, railroad artifacts, and memorabilia—is open for visiting.

If you're not a cold-weather person, you can still climb aboard these antique iron horses during the museum's Railfest, held over the Memorial Day weekend, and on Autumn Color Trains, the first two full weekends in October, when the Baraboo River Valley, woodlands, and rolling farm fields are ablaze with fall colors.

For More Information

Mid-Continent Railway Museum is located about five miles west of Baraboo on State 136, then less than three miles southwest on County PF. During the museum's regular season, mid-May through Labor Day, four steam-train trips are offered daily, rain or shine. For more information, contact the museum at North Freedom, WI 53951, 608-522-4261.

215

47

Snowo Dynamo

ST. GERMAIN

WINTER IN THE NORTH WOODS HAS A SPECIAL APPEAL. Picture huge stands of virgin pines sprinkled with glistening white snow. Patches of white birch sparkle in the winter sunshine. Fir trees stand so tall they seem to pierce the clouds.

The snow season also transforms these northern climes into a snowmobiler's paradise. A network of snowmobile trails covers hundreds of miles, magically crisscrossing scenic woodlands and connecting tiny neighboring villages (former lumber towns with charming names like Star Lake, Arbor Vitae, and St. Germain) with well-marked trails, groomed regularly by area snowmobile clubs. Not to mention the numberless "pit stops"—toasty pubs and roadside saloons along the trail that cater almost exclusively in winter months to hearty sledders.

From the first snows in late November to the last weeks of March, the roar of snowmobiles echoes through North Woods forests. Sled enthusiasm in these parts borders on fanaticism. Snowmobilers think nothing of traveling hundreds of miles a day, slashing through dense forests in the glinty winter sun or enjoying an evening caravan through the woods by moonlight.

It's kind of like a slice of "Northern Exposure" come to life.

North Woods snowmobiling is steeped in a history almost as deep as its powdery snow. In 1924 Carl Eliason, of Sayner, built the first machine-powered sled. He patented the sled three years later and manufactured 40 of them. After receiving an order from Finland for 200 sleds, Eliason sold the patent. Today more than 2.5 million snowmobiles buzz around North America, with nearly nine million people enjoying the winter activity. When Eliason died at 80 in December 1979, his funeral procession consisted of a mile-long parade of snowmobiles.

Winter

St. Germain is the headquarters for North Woods "snomo" adventures in these parts. Local dealers rent machines and helmets for a few hours or several days. Some even offer guided tours ranging from three to seven days and including meals and accommodations. Whatever your choice, be sure to wear a snowmobile suit (or heavy ski suit) over layered clothing, thick mittens, and heavy boots to withstand some frigid temperatures made worse by speeding through the woods at up to 30 mph.

The town is located on the southeastern tip of one of Wisconsin's best snowmobile areas—the Northern Highland–American Legion State Forest. Covering more than 200,000 wilderness acres, the forest offers more than 75 miles of official snowmobile trails that connect with an extensive network of county and local club trails, adding on hundreds of extra miles to the "snow highway."

Count on seeing wildlife despite the noise. On my last winter tour in these parts, an owl remained perched in a tree while our entire 10-sled party passed his lofty home. We also saw a porcupine waddling through deep drifts and a herd of deer, which was curiously calm as they watched our sleds roar by.

However, you don't have to visit the North Woods for snowmobile fun. Wisconsin boasts more than 25,000 miles of interconnected snow trails, stretching from the tops of ancient mountains and granite bluffs to sunlit meadows and winter-carved lakeside landscapes. What did you expect from the state that invented the contraption in the first place?

FOR MORE INFORMATION

Rentals and tours are available through St. Germain Rental/Tours, 6255 Highway 70 East, St. Germain, WI 54558, 715-479-8007; Decker's Snow-Venture Tours, P.O. Box 1447, Eagle River, WI 54521, 715-479-2764.

For more Wisconsin snowmobiling information, contact Northern Highlands–American Legion State Forest, P.O. Box 440, Woodruff, WI 54568, 715-356-5211; Wisconsin Tourism Development, P.O. Box 7606, Madison, WI 53707, 800-372-2737 (Wisconsin and adjacent states) or 800-432-8747 (nationally).

Snow Dynamo

48

U-Chop Xmas Trees

DELAVAN

YULE BE GLAD TO KNOW THAT THERE ARE PLENTY OF PLACES in Wisconsin where you can chop down your own Christmas tree again this year. But you'd better hurry. Christmas Day arrives sooner than you think.

At least it always seems that way. Actually, you've got plenty of time if you go by international standards. Several western European cultures, such as Austria's, traditionally never even bring out the family tree until Christmas Eve.

Even early American settlers saved tree trimming for the night before Christmas, stringing together simple decorations like popcorn and cranberries and hanging homemade paper ornaments, chains, stars, and wax candles in tin holders from the branches.

And speaking of decorations, did you know that the custom of bedecking trees came from Germany? Seems evergreens always have been a symbol used in European winter celebrations. But it wasn't until the eighth century that St. Boniface, a German monk, suggested people decorate fir trees to honor the birth of baby Jesus.

Enough trivia. Off we go to chop down the family Christmas tree. Remember that a cut-your-own tree expedition is great family fun provided you're prepared for the weather. So here are a few guidelines:

- Dress warmly in layered clothes, because open fields and woodlands might be chilly even on mild, sunny days. Wear insulated, waterproof boots and gloves (deerskin mittens are best). And your mother was right: wear a hat.

- Though many tree farms provide handsaws for tree toppers, bring your own along so you won't have to wait to use one. And pack plenty of rope to tie the tree down.

- A tree is probably fresh if it doesn't drop tons of needles when the trunk is thumped on the ground or if you can pinch needles on a branch and watch them spring back (rather than fall off).

- When you get home, remember to cut one to one and a half inches from the tree trunk, and set the tree in a bucket of water for 12 hours. Live trees need lots of moisture to stay fresh, so water yours daily.

Winter

- Be sure to phone ahead and check on tree-farm hours and the availability of the tree variety you desire. And ask for detailed directions to the tree farm before you leave home!

You shouldn't have any trouble finding a tree at Ron Piening's Harmas Farms in Delevan. Piening boasts three different Christmas tree plantations, all within a few minutes of each other—and they total nearly 70,000 trees.

"I've been operating tree plantations for about 20 years now," Piening said. "So it seems like we should have something for everybody."

Piening's plantations feature Fraser firs, Norway spruce, Colorado blue spruce, balsam, fir, scotch pine, and white pine. "Many run up to 10 or 12 feet tall," Piening said. "But you also can find plenty of six- and seven-footers, too."

Cost for any size is $45. Bring your own saws. "We have some loaners, but if we're busy, you might have to wait a while to use them," Piening advised. He'll provide twine for tie-downs.

Cut-your-own plantations are open weekends (Friday through Sunday), from 9:00 A.M. to 7:00 P.M.

To get there, Piening suggests you take Northwest Highway (Route 14) into Wisconsin and continue about 15 miles across the Illinois-Wisconsin state line until reaching Wisconsin 89; go north on 89 for one mile; at R & D Town Line Road, go right for a half-mile until reaching Plantation I. For more information call 800-728-8898.

Another good choice is Paul's Tree Farm in Brodhead. It's worth the ride to south-central Wisconsin for these beautiful trees, which include everything from white, Norway, and Scotch pines to Black Hills pines and blue spruce. Call 608-897-2569 or check out the farm's website at http://user.mc.net/pinetree.

FOR MORE INFORMATION

For more Wisconsin U-chop Christmas-tree farms, call Wisconsin's Department of Tourism at 800-432-8747.

U-Chop Xmas Trees

49

An American Club Christmas

KOHLER

I PEEKED INTO THE FORMAL LIBRARY TO DISCOVER CHRISTMAS carols being sung in front of a roaring fire. But this songfest really got into the *spirit* of things. Singers included gentlemen dressed in top hats and fancy velvet waistcoats; ladies were gussied up in long Victorian gowns and festive bonnets. Guests also nibbled on holiday cookies while drinking mulled cider and tea. It was a scene right out of Charles Dickens. But I was in Kohler, an enchanted village about an hour's drive north of Milwaukee.

Such scenes are typical at the American Club, Wisconsin's only five-diamond resort, and one of the Midwest's most luxurious getaways. Its special holiday magic transports you back to a long-ago time of horse-drawn carriage rides and elegant surroundings. The resort itself resembles a sprawling baronial estate, backlit by 180,000 tiny white Christmas lights that sparkle whisper-soft on the Wisconsin snowscape.

Inside, guest rooms glisten with handcarved oak trimmings, skylit rooms, and whirlpool baths (made by Kohler, renowned plumbing manufacturers, of course) whose styles range from luxurious, marble-columned retreats fit for the Rockefellers to enclosed habitat chambers where weather (wind, rain, and sun) is at your fingertip control.

After your first holiday visit you may think that grand Christmas traditions originated here. Seasonal charms include everything from afternoon teas and gourmet holiday dining to wreath-making workshops and Christmas tree trimming. And there's plenty doing for kids, too.

December weekends offer their own holiday happenings. Walk into the courtyard and down the garden path to the hotel's antique stained-glass greenhouse, imported from England and reconstructed piece by piece on this site. It provides afternoon teas (also offered daily, mid-December through January 1) featuring such British delicacies as Aunt Rachel's scones and Bakewell tarts. Additional weekend fun includes Christmas decoration workshops, live music, and dancing.

Other times, Santa himself gets into the act. On designated weekends, you'll shake hands with jolly Saint Nick as he personally greets guests in the hotel lobby during late afternoon and early evening check-ins. Dickens-era costumed caroling in the library also begins mid-December and continues to Christmas Eve.

Serious Christmas lovers should get ready for the second and third weekends of December, which present a mother lode of holiday gems. Adults can count on afternoon teas, seafood buffets, floral workshops, music, and dancing. For kids, each Saturday arrives with "Breakfast with Santa," children's floral-decoration workshops, Mrs. Claus's Cookie Workshop, the Christmas story lady (at the nearby Shops at Woodlake), Christmas caroling, and both afternoon and evening sessions of holiday movies.

Holiday revelers who can sneak away midweek or take a long weekend might consider one of the American Club's premier events—"In Celebration of Chocolate," slated for a Thursday evening in mid-December. This one-night extravaganza is the ultimate indulgence for chocoholics.

Elegant buffet tables are laden with exquisite gourmet

chocolate masterpieces concocted by the hotel's pastry chef and crew; the rest is up to you and your waistline. Count on sampling among thousands of truffles and hundreds of tortes, cakes, and confections. Admission is charged, with special "chocolate" packages available.

Christmas Eve at the American Club has its own traditions. Fun kicks off with a teddy bear picnic lunch for kids; little ones are encouraged to bring along their favorite cuddly friends. Then children head for the library to help trim an old-fashioned Christmas tree. They can cut and paste paper chains, create special ornaments, or string together the cranberries and popcorn that are heaped on tables.

Later that afternoon is the Bûche de Noël Caroling Reception and Christmas Book Sign-In, followed by a gourmet Christmas Eve feast at the Immigrant, the hotel's signature restaurant.

Christmas Day offers its Olde English Christmas Dinner (reservations required), as well as a holiday champagne reception.

If that's not enough holiday festivities for you, venture down the road to the Shops at Woodlake, which offer boutiques, Christmas workshops, demonstrations, and musical performances at various times throughout the season.

Try tennis, swimming, or a workout at the Sports Core, the hotel's indoor sporting complex that's just a short walk or shuttlebus ride away.

You also can cross-country ski, toboggan, or just take a hike through the snow at River Wildlife, a 500-acre preserve that sets aside some of the most pristine Wisconsin wilderness imaginable for American Club guests. It's your passport to a private winter wonderland.

An American Club Christmas

For More Information

Several Christmas events (including dinners and teas) require reservations and additional fees. For reservations or information, contact The American Club, Highland Drive, Kohler, WI 53044, 920-457-8000 or 800-344-2838.

Winter

50

Nordic Nirvana

THERE IS A SPECIAL SOUND HEARD BY CROSS-COUNTRY SKIERS: the poetry of silence. And it's accompanied by the stark beauty of gnarled trees swaying before arctic gusts, tracks of porcupine and field mice frozen in the pure white snow, thawed punch holes made by deer.

Cross-country terrain is a magical world pulsing with the serenity of life in the winter wilds. And it is this sense of tranquility, simplicity, and leisurely touring that has ignited the Nordic ski boom. Wisconsin, with more than 300 Nordic facilities, claims some of the best terrain for Midwest cross-country adventures. Touring centers get even better as you go farther north, with a greater variety of trails, spectacular North Woods scenery, and dramatic winter lakeshore landscapes.

Many offer groomed, tracked, and set trails, clearly marked for all skill levels and regularly patrolled by ski rescue teams. There are boundless opportunities for off-trail adventures that can incorporate winter camping expeditions along Great Lakes shores.

Let's not forget moonlight skiing, Nordic schools, wax clinics, races, demonstrations, and ski packages that might include lodging, trail passes, instruction, meals, and entertainment. Choices are endless, but here are two of my cross-country favorites.

Winter Park & Nordic Center, in Minocqua, is a premier cross-country touring outpost sometimes used by Olympic-caliber athletes for training and practice. Situated in the heart of the North Woods, Winter Park offers miles of trails winding through lush forests, over challenging hills, and along breathtaking clearings.

I'll never forget my last Nordic adventure here, when temperatures dipped to 10 below zero, turning my mustache into a mass of icicles. But constant motion kept me comfortably warm. I marveled at little things, like the crazy snow etchings made by pine needles flung by strong winds, the deep silence of the woods, and the power of the wilderness setting. It was great.

Winter Park has a heated chalet, ski shop, rentals, ski school, and snack bar serving hot drinks and carbo-loading treats. For information, contact the center at Box 22, Minocqua, WI 54548, 715-356-3309.

Maybe you want to ski right out the door of a quaint country inn and into a winter wonderland? Then try Door County, which boasts several inns at the doorstep of Nordic adventures. For an inn listing or winter activity guide, contact Door County Chamber of Commerce, Box 219, Sturgeon Bay, WI 54235, 920-743-4456.

One of the most spectacular treks covers the 30 miles of groomed trails (all skill levels) at Peninsula State Park on State 42 near Ephraim. You will see snow-dusted pine, hemlock forests, and the dramatic ice-encrusted shoreline of Lake Michigan. There is a one-day, out-of-state vehicle entry fee at state parks.

A good time for those interested in learning Nordic touring skills is mid-January's Wisconsin Cross-Country Ski Week. For seven days, more than 20 statewide cross-country areas offer special events, lessons, and programs to put you into the Nordic touring groove.

For More Information

To receive a complete list of state cross-country facilities, contact Wisconsin Division of Tourism, P.O. Box 7606, Madison, WI 53707, 800-432-8747.

Nordic Nirvana

51

Eagle Watching

PRAIRIE DU CHIEN AND PRAIRIE DU SAC

FOR MANY PEOPLE IN WISCONSIN, WINTER MEANS MORE THAN cold weather, icy winds, and mounds of snow. It means heading out into the wild to witness bald eagles soaring above the open water of the Mississippi and Wisconsin Rivers, circling their wintering grounds in a spectacle of winter wildlife unmatched almost anywhere in the Midwest.

Migratory waterfowl experts say that the stretch of Mississippi River along Wisconsin's southwestern border holds North America's largest populations of wintering eagles. People are often overwhelmed by their numbers. But there's a whole lot of wilderness in the Midwest that people aren't aware of.

From the end of November to mid-March, nearly 200 eagles winter in Prairie du Chien. You have to get right along the river for the best sights of eagles fishing along the Mississippi and foraging for food in surrounding bottomlands.

For a "total immersion" eagle-watching tour, wind your way along the Mississippi from Rock Island, Illinois, to Prairie du Chien; stop at Wisconsin's Wyalusing State Park (one of the Midwest's most beautiful spots, with bluffs overlooking the confluence of the Mississippi and Wisconsin Rivers); then explore eagle hot spots along the Wisconsin and drive through eagle-occupied farm fields and bottomlands, until finally winding back down along the Mississippi to your starting point at Prairie du Chien.

Eagle-watching tours do not have to be rugged; in fact, anyone who loves the outdoors and is in decent shape will find it a breeze. Be sure to dress warmly (layers of clothing are best, with a good pair of thick-soled hiking boots) and bring along binoculars. You can't get too close to the birds without them getting skittish and flying away. Even the sound of a slamming car door can drive them away.

Don't forget photography equipment to capture some of these nature sights on film. Gadgets like a telephoto, telescopic, and wide-angle lens are musts for good pictures.

If you'd rather look for eagles while leaving the driving (and climbing and hiking) to someone else, head to Prairie du Sac (near Madison) for its annual mid-January Eagle Watch Festival. Besides great guided bus tours to three prime eagle-gathering locations along the Wisconsin River, the wildlife weekend includes naturalist-led raptor seminars, wine tasting, and kids' activities.

For More Information

For more eagle-watching information, contact Sauk-Prairie Chamber of Commerce, P.O. Box 7, Sauk City, WI 53583, 608-634-4168; Prairie du Chien Chamber of Commerce, 211 South Main Street, P.O. Box 326, Prairie du Chien, WI 53821, 800-732-1673.

52

Winter Camping

WINTER CAMPING IS DIFFERENT. BASICALLY, YOU SLEEP OUT-side in the cold.

However, winter camping is surging in popularity, riding the crest of high-tech advances in cold-weather gear and the "return to wilderness" movement.

It's easy to find a place to stretch out in Wisconsin. About 15 state and national forests boast two million acres of winter wilderness to explore. Your only restriction is your ability to get there.

You won't simply stare at frozen tundra. Why not camp out near snow-covered bluffs overlooking an icy river or take a short hike from a shoreline whipped into a labyrinth of sea caves? Maybe a meadow muffled in winter white and surrounded by tall green pines is more your style. Here are my two favorite winter camping hot spots:

Newport State Park, located five miles northeast of Ellison Bay, on State 42 in Door County, is one of the most scenic wilderness areas in Wisconsin's state park system. Once the site of an old logging village (the ruins of loggers' cabins can still be found in the woods), Newport boasts backpack camping at 16 secluded sites strung from one to three and a half miles from the main parking lot. Believe me, that's plenty of distance during a Door County winter.

Cold-season adventures include cross-country skiing on 23 miles of informal trails, snowshoe trekking, and ice fishing on Europe Lake, an inland body of water within the park.

Best winter vistas are along the park's 11 miles of Lake Michigan shoreline. Huge ice sheets might be stacked atop one another like cold-weather shelves. And from low sea cliffs, tongues of ice snake from craggy outcroppings down to the waters below. Just remember, this is winter camping at its toughest. No water is available here; it must be carried in and out. Also there's no electricity.

Wyalusing, State Park, six miles south of Prairie du Chien on U.S. 18, then six miles west on County C, is perched atop

bluffs more than 500 feet high overlooking the confluence of the Mississippi and Wisconsin Rivers. Its winter wonders include lofty river bluffs, snow-dappled Indian mounds, and panoramic vistas.

The rivers also are important wintering grounds for bald eagles. From November to March (January is prime time) winter campers can carefully scale bluff-top aeries to watch these majestic birds soar through the sky or dive into icy waters for their fishy cold-weather meal.

There are 132 campsites with electrical outlets; also count on flush toilets and showers. Enjoy three and a half miles of groomed and tracked cross-country ski trails, ice fishing, and sledding. Snowshoers can trek over 14 miles of hiking trails.

If you're planning a winter camping expedition, keep these points in mind:

Campsite Selection Best spot is a flat clearing in a wooded area, surrounded by tall trees to shield you from winds. In open terrain, pitch your tent crosswind to eliminate the possibility of snowdrifts inundating you. Also stay away from hillsides that could create dangerous snowslides.

Tent Breathable synthetic fibers help the tent ward off wind, keep the heat, and allow air to circulate. Floors and sidewalls should be waterproof, and a water-resistant fly should cover the outside of the tent. Roofs should be steeply pitched to avoid snow buildup.

Sleeping Bags The shell should be ripstop nylon, which is water resistant while allowing air to pass. Bags filled with prime northern goose down or insulated with synthetic Dacron 11 and Holofil 11 are among the best. A good bag should also have a Derlin zipper or something similar that won't freeze. You also need a mat to insulate against the snow and cold ground.

Clothes Dress in layers to trap body heat while allowing moisture to evaporate—polypropylene underwear, wool pants, shirt, sweater, and socks, and a down-filled jacket are paramount. Mittens store heat better than finger gloves; deerskin are best, lined with wool or silk. Essential is a loose-fitting, wind-resistant parka with a hood and with waist and wrist cords to keep out drafts. Boots should be waterproofed with wool or synthetic liners. Dry them every evening. Also wear a hat, a knit cap that can be pulled over the ears or a hat with earflaps that ties around the chin. Face masks, balaclavas, and scarves add layered protection against a frostbitten face.

Food Your body needs more energy in cold weather, especially if you're cross-country skiing, hiking, snowshoeing, or engaging in strenuous activity. Gorp (dried fruit, nuts, raisins, and chocolate bits) is good for snacking. Meals can be served from freeze-dried packs containing chicken, beef,

Winter Camping

and ham; these need only to be boiled. Packets of instant soup, cheese, dry sausage, and peanut butter are good energy providers. You'll also need lots of liquids—water, hot chocolate, juices, soups, broths. Avoid alcohol; it gives you a false sense of warmth while dulling other senses.

Fuel Your campsite should include a double-burner pressure camp stove run by gas or butane. Gas won't freeze, but butane might get slushy in extreme cold. So you may have to place the canister in a sleeping bag at night. Check with park rangers to see if campfires are allowed.

First Aid and Emergencies Essentials are maps, compass, extra food and clothing, flashlight, matches, firestarter, candle, knife, sunglasses, and a first-aid kit. In an emergency, stay calm, think clearly, devise a plan, and stick to it. If you lose your way without a compass, turn your watch so the hour hand points at the sun—true south lies halfway between the hour hand and twelve. Many emergencies can be avoided by traveling with a companion or telling someone your travel plans.

Be especially watchful for frostbite and hypothermia. Minor frostbite can be treated by placing a bare hand or finger on the frozen spot or putting a frozen finger under the armpit. Best treatment for frozen feet is to place bare feet on someone's warm tummy.

Hypothermia is the number one killer of outdoor recreationists. Symptoms of hypothermia (severe loss of body heat) are uncontrollable shivers, slurred speech, poor coordination, and exhaustion. For treatment, build a fire and immediately get out of wet clothes and into a warm sleeping bag. In extreme cases, get someone to lie in the sleeping bag with the victim to provide body heat. Also provide frequent sips of warm liquids and bits of high-energy foods.

Winter

FOR MORE INFORMATION

For a list of winter camping sites, contact Wisconsin Department of Natural Resources, Bureau of Parks & Recreation, P.O. Box 7921, Madison, WI 53707, 608-266-2181; Newport State Park, 415 South County Highway NP, Ellison Bay, WI 54210, 920-854-2500; Wyalusing State Park, 13342 County Highway C, Bagley, WI 53801, 608-996-2261.

Winter Camping

Index